Events That Changed the Course of History:

The Story of the Russian Revolution 100 Years Later

Jessica E. Piper

EVENTS THAT CHANGED THE COURSE OF HISTORY: THE STORY OF THE RUSSIAN REVOLUTION 100 YEARS LATER
Copyright © 2016 Atlantic Publishing Group, Inc.

1405 SW 6th Avenue • Ocala, Florida 34471 • Phone 800-814-1132 • Fax 352-622-1875
Web site: www.atlantic-pub.com • Email: sales@atlantic-pub.com
SAN Number: 268-1250

Library of Congress Cataloging-in-Publication Data

Names: Piper, Jessica E., 1994- author.
Title: Events that changed the course of history : the story of the Russian
    Revolution 100 years later / by Jessica E. Piper.
Description: Ocala, Florida : Atlantic Publishing Group, Inc., 2016. |
    Includes bibliographical references and index.
Identifiers: LCCN 2016040826| ISBN 9781620231432 (alkaline paper) | ISBN
    1620231433 (alkaline paper) | ISBN 9781620231500 (electronic)
Subjects: LCSH: Soviet Union--History--Revolution, 1917-1921. | Soviet
    Union--History--Revolution, 1917-1921--Influence. |
    Russia--History--February Revolution, 1917.
Classification: LCC DK265 .P473 2016 | DDC 947.084/1--dc23 LC record available at https://lccn.
loc.gov/2016040826

PROJECT MANAGER: Rebekah Sack • rsack@atlantic-pub.com
ASSISTANT EDITOR: Taylor Gaines • taylorgaines26@gmail.com
INTERIOR LAYOUT AND JACKET DESIGN: Steven W. Booth • steven@geniusbookcompany.com
COVER DESIGN: Jackie Miller • sullmill@charter.net

Photo Credits: Image(s) or Footage (as applicable), used under license from Shutterstock.com.
Hammer and sickle icon: Used under Creative Commons Attribution Share Alike 3.0 license, created by user Superloosha. https://commons.wikimedia.org/wiki/File:Communism.png

Reduce. Reuse.
RECYCLE.

A decade ago, Atlantic Publishing signed the Green Press Initiative. These guidelines promote environmentally friendly practices, such as using recycled stock and vegetable-based inks, avoiding waste, choosing energy-efficient resources, and promoting a no-pulping policy. We now use 100-percent recycled stock on all our books. The results: in one year, switching to post-consumer recycled stock saved 24 mature trees, 5,000 gallons of water, the equivalent of the total energy used for one home in a year, and the equivalent of the greenhouse gases from one car driven for a year.

Over the years, we have adopted a number of dogs from rescues and shelters. First there was Bear and after he passed, Ginger and Scout. Now, we have Kira, another rescue. They have brought immense joy and love not just into our lives, but into the lives of all who met them.

We want you to know a portion of the profits of this book will be donated in Bear, Ginger and Scout's memory to local animal shelters, parks, conservation organizations, and other individuals and nonprofit organizations in need of assistance.

– Douglas & Sherri Brown,
President & Vice-President of Atlantic Publishing

Contents

Foreword

History itself made me want to learn more about Russia. Perhaps history first grabbed me when I was a boy rummaging through old pictures and documents in my grandparents' steamer trunk, brought with them from China when they came to California in the 1930s. Or perhaps it was when kids in school wondered how my mother could be born in China but not be Chinese — so I got used to telling the history of how my mother's parents left Russia in 1909, took a ship to New York City hoping for a better life, worked in garment factories, returned to visit their parents in the summer of 1914 when my grandfather was drafted into the Russian army and sent to the front, tried to return to America after the tsar was overthrown but went through China because the war in Europe was still going on, found they could live well in the Russia community in Harbin, and fled again to America with three children in 1939 to escape Japanese occupation and the approach of a new world war. In high school, these family stories mixed with bigger Cold War stories about the evils of communism and about Russia as the greatest threat to our freedom and security. All these stories made me ask more questions.

Thinking about these stories, I wanted to know not only how the present grew out of the past, but what the past meant to people, like my family, who lived that history. One idea about the study of history is that it is mainly about causes and effects, how the world got to where it is. But I began to lean toward a different idea about the study of history: that it should also be about how people lived and experienced history as it was happening to them and as they tried to make it happen. It is this way of studying history — as people's lived experiences (though this was not usually what I got in school) — that inspired me to become a historian.

So, when I think of the Russian Revolution, I think of the stories of the thousands of individuals whose lives and words I have encountered in studying those times. Of course, as a historian, I look for patterns, explanations, and trends. But these individual human stories also remind me how messy and complex that past was for those living it. The author of this book, Jessica Piper, is right: the "story of the Russian Revolution" is the stories of the many different types of people she describes, from the tsar to revolutionary leaders to ordinary citizens.

The story of the revolution was certainly found in the lives of leaders like Lev (Leon) Trotsky. You will meet him in the pages following as the organizer of the October 1917 takeover of government power, as the leader of the Red Army during the Civil War, and as the enemy and victim of Stalin. But he was also an idealist, a dreamer, a romantic, like so many revolutionaries. As a teenager living in a provincial town, he was moved by the passion of socialist exiles he met there, and he decided to become a revolutionary himself — resulting in his arrest and exile to Siberia at the age of 19. His dream for himself, in his words, was to "fight for a future…when man, strong and beautiful, will master the drifting stream of history and direct it towards the boundless horizon of beauty, joy, and happiness!"[1]

Later, as head of the Red Army, he was responsible for a great deal of brutal violence. But he was determined to see it as not only "necessary" to defend the government against its enemies, but as good and righteous, as part of that dream. Yes, we practice dictatorship, he admitted in response to critics of Communist rule, but we do this to end the causes of dictatorship; yes, we use violence and terror, but in order to end all violence; yes, we "violate the sacredness of human life," but in order to "destroy the social order that crucifies the human being."[2] Perhaps he was wrong to think that the end justifies the means. But his faith in the beauty of those ends inspired him as they inspired so many others at the time. He remained a romantic about revolution after the Civil War ended in victor, imagining the transformed human being of the communist future: "the average human type will rise to the heights of an Aristotle, a Goethe, or a Marx. And above this ridge new peaks will rise."[3]

Another dreamer you will briefly encounter is Alexandra Kollontai. As Commissar (Minister) of Social Welfare, she was probably the highest-ranking woman in government anywhere in the world up to that time. She began her political life as a young woman declaring to her parents that she would not marry for money and position, as was expected of upper-class women, but only "out of a great passion." Soon, she turned away from the traditional life of housewife to become a writer. Like so many young Russians at the start of the 20th century, she was attracted to socialism as a vision of a more just society for everyone. But unlike most socialists of her time, she insisted that transforming the personal lives of women was as important as getting them to join the political struggle. Indeed, the personal and the political could not be separated, she insisted.

She annoyed and even shocked most socialist men by writing mainly about women, sex, and love: about women being treated as inferior and feeling themselves inferior, and about women not finding satisfaction, emotionally or physically, in their relationships. This mattered politically, she insisted, for it was not men who were to blame, but a society built on inequality and on values other than a full and happy life for every individual. If a revolution did not transform everything in life, it would not be a true revolution. Personally and politically, she disliked Trotsky. But they shared the same dream.

Of course, the story of the revolution is not only the stories of leaders. Most of its stories are those of ordinary people, especially the millions of workers and peasants you will also hear about in this book. Their *collective* lives and actions made history, as you will hear. But I think of the *individual* stories they told in letters sent to people in power during the days of revolution in 1917:

A peasant named Martynov, for example, wrote a long letter to the government that replaced the tsar explaining why all the land should immediately be given to the farmers who work it because allowing landlords to continue owning big estates is immoral: "the land we share is our mother; she feeds us and gives us shelter; she makes us happy and lovingly warms us… Selling land created by the Heavenly Creator is a barbaric absurdity."[4]

A soldier at the front wrote to plead with "comrade workers and soldiers" back home to stop talking all the time and do something, for "we're sitting in the trenches without light or happiness… We're all sick and have no strength left… We've had enough bloodshed. We must end the war no matter what. If they want an offensive, then we'll mount an offensive against the capitalists and bourgeoisie who are drowning us and killing our freedom."[5]

A worker wrote to complain that the new leaders, even those who called themselves revolutionaries and socialists, are liars who only pretend to care about ordinary working people. "The leaders of our revolutionary movement… shout at the top of their lungs that 'the chains have been broken and freedom has come!' But, damn it, what kind of freedom is it when millions of voiceless slaves are still being led like sheep to the cannons and machine guns… If you really want good, happiness, and all the rest for the people, then climb down off the people's mighty back, which you have been riding on and squeezing all the juice from."[6]

There are so many stories and voices like these. As the author of this book says, so many of these point to the widespread "dream" for an "equal, just society," though there were many different ideas of what "justice" meant. This is a dream we find throughout world history. It was certainly at the heart of the history of what the Russian Revolution meant for so many.

That this was not how things turned out made many supporters of the revolution frustrated and angry, like the Kronstadt rebels in 1921 whose suppression (by Trotsky!) opens this book, and like the worker who wrote to the new Communist leaders in 1918 to tell them they were all "imposters" pretending to be for workers and peasants when really they were "crucifying freedom" just like the tsar did.[7]

Perhaps, history is mostly a story of dreams and disappointments. Certainly, we see this in the long history of the Russian Revolution. But for me, what really makes the study of history powerful is that people keep dreaming and believing despite all the evidence that the scales of history are weighted toward disappointment. This is a very human story. Enjoy exploring it.

—Mark D. Steinberg

Mark D. Steinberg teaches history at the University of Illinois. He is the author of many books and articles, including "A History of Russia" with the late Nicholas Riasanovsky (he is now working on the ninth edition) and three books on the Russian Revolution, all for students and general readers, "The Fall of the Romanovs" (Yale University Press, 1995), "Voices of Revolution" (Yale University Press, 2001), and "The Russian Revolution, 1905-1921" (Oxford University Press, 2017).

Sources

1. From a newspaper essay he wrote for *Vostochnoe obozrenie* (Eastern Observer), published 17 February 1901.

2. Trotsky, *Terrorism and Communism* (1920).

3. Trotsky, *Literature and Revolution* (1923).

4. Letter from Semyon Martynov to the government, August 1917, State Archive of the Russian Federation, fond 1778, op. 1, d. 234, ll. 88-89ob.

5. "Voice from the Trenches," 30 May 1917, State Archive of the Russian Federation, f. 1244, op. 2, d. 10, ll. 177-78.

6. Letter from A. Zemskov to Minister of Justice Alexander Kerensky, 26 March 1917, State Archive of the Russian Federation, f. 6978, op. 1, d. 296, ll. 39-45ob.

7. Letter from F. Petrov to the Central Executive Committee of Soviets, January 1918, State Archive of the Russian Federation, f. 1235, op. 40, d. 8, ll. 97-97b.

Introduction

The date was March 7, 1921, and the sound of heavy artillery could be heard in the Russian city of Petrograd. Communist forces were preparing a dangerous attack on the nearby military fort of Kronstadt. The next day, soldiers would run across a five-mile-long sheet of ice in an attempt to raid the fort. To make the attack a surprise, the soldiers at the front of the army covered themselves in white bedsheets.[1]

Navy ships in the port of present-day Kronstadt.

1   Figes, 763.

Why were communist forces attacking the fort at Kronstadt? The Kronstadt sailors were Russians too, and had once been loyal communists. When the Russian Revolution began in 1917, they had helped take down Russia's tsar.

But that was four years earlier. The Kronstadt sailors felt betrayed by the new communist government, and now they were preparing to fight it. Holed up in their fort, they wrote a rally song, expressing their displeasure with the course of events.

"We shook off the Romanovs, and got the communists instead," one verse went.[2]

When the communists attacked the next day, the sailors fought back. Their machine gun fire broke the ice, and thousands of communist soldiers fell into the freezing water, where they drowned. But the sailor's resistance was short-lived. After several days of fighting, the communists did ultimately take down Kronstadt. Hundreds — possibly thousands — of sailors were executed.

The episode between the Kronstadt sailors and the communist soldiers was one of many battles in the loosely-defined Russian Civil War. But it was also a fight about the meaning of the Russian Revolution. The sailors saw themselves as true revolutionaries who had been betrayed by the government. The communists saw the sailors as "counterrevolutionaries" who were trying to undo the gains that Russia had made.

---

2   Daly and Trofminov, 291.

These contradictions, and the bloodshed that accompanied them, are central to the tale of Russia's struggle.

In this book, you will read about people who died fighting to bring communism to Russia, and you will read about people who died as a result of the communist regime. You will read about an incompetent tsar whose polices tore millions of families apart, yet who — in the year before his death — only wanted to enjoy a normal life with his wife and children. You will read about leaders who changed the course of history, and about millions of everyday citizens whose lives were forever changed by events that they could not control.

All of these stories are the story of the Russian Revolution.

Chapter 1: Backwards Russia

On a cold day in November 1894, in a bedroom of the Livadia Palace, a young man named Nicholas was crying. Nicholas was not a typical 26-year-old. He was the heir to the Russian throne, and he had gathered with his family and a team of doctors at the palace because his father, Alexander III, was dying of kidney disease. When Alexander passed away a few hours later, the crying man would become Tsar Nicholas II, the supreme leader of the Russian empire. He was worried about his prospects.

"What is going to happen to me and to all of Russia?" Nicholas said to his cousin. "I am not prepared to be a tsar."[1]

Nicholas had reasons to be afraid. The empire he would inherit was facing many challenges. While the rest of the world seemed to be modernizing, Russia was stuck in the past. Most of its people were farmers, but farming in Russia was difficult. The Russian military, lacking in technology and resources, was unprepared for conflict. And the government — even the very presence of the tsar — seemed outdated, as many countries were shifting to more democratic structures.

1   Figes, 18.

Livadia Palace in Yalta, Crimea.

Russia saw these challenges when Nicholas became tsar in 1894. Just 23 years later, the empire would erupt in revolution. What would happen to Nicholas? The answer was not good. What would happen to Russia? The country would never be the same.

The Tsar

The system of government that brought Nicholas into power was already outdated when the new tsar was crowned. The Russian empire was a hereditary monarchy, meaning that power was passed from one member of the royal family to the next. Additionally, the Russian tsar was an autocrat, meaning he had absolute power. While most European countries had a parliament or a representative body, Nicholas got to make all of the decisions himself.

The Romanovs

Tsar Nicholas II was the member of the House of Romanov, which had ruled Russia since 1613. Over the years, the Romanov rulers had encountered plenty of crises, but they had always managed to keep control over the empire. Though Nicholas came from this same bloodline, he wasn't ready to rule Russia.

The royal family

Baby-faced and naturally shy, Tsar Nicholas II was known as Nicky to most of his family members. He was very religious, a member of the Russian Orthodox Church. By most historical accounts, Nicholas cared deeply about his family. Following Romanov traditions, he married a foreign princess, Alexandra, who was born in Germany. Together, the couple had four daughters and one son. Their son, Alexei, had hemophilia, a genetic disorder that prevented his blood from clotting normally, which meant he could bleed to death even from a small cut.

Alexandra was deeply protective of her only son. Following his birth in 1904, she didn't make very many public appearances, leading many ordinary Russians to believe that she was cold or uncaring. In an attempt to find a cure for Alexei, she hired Grigori Rasputin, a mysterious man from Western Siberia who claimed to have healing powers. Though many outsiders distrusted Rasputin — he was a known drunkard and was accused of much worse — the royal family continued to keep him as an advisor.

Not fit to rule

Although Nicholas was generally regarded as intelligent and well-educated, he wasn't particularly interested in politics. He was thrust into the role of tsar unexpectedly — his father's illness and death happened out of nowhere. Just a month before he became the tsar, Nicholas had written a long entry in his diary about an epic chestnut-throwing battle that he had engaged in with Prince George of Greece.[2]

Nicholas also lacked his father's forceful personality. He didn't like making big decisions, especially when other people were around. He worried about being impolite to the point where he would quietly agree with people, rather than daring to contradict them when his opinion differed. As a result, many people who knew the tsar quickly came to view him as weak. Certain members of Russian high society even questioned if Nicholas was truly making decisions himself, or if he was controlled by someone else. (Some suspected Rasputin, although they were probably incorrect).

Despite these flaws, Nicholas did try to govern. He occupied much of his time with relatively trivial tasks, like managing individual budgets of far-off agricultural schools or reading minor petitions to the Chancellery. By keeping himself busy,

2   Figes, 17.

Nicholas may have thought his country was running smoothly. Unfortunately for him, that quickly proved not to be the case.

Fast Fact: In imperial Russia, peasants needed permission from the tsar to change their names. Nicholas received hundreds of petitions each month from peasants whose unfortunate nicknames — which meant things like "ugly" or "smelly" — had been formalized as legal names.[3]

Farming Society

In terms of sheer size, the Russian empire was the largest in the world. Spanning from Eastern Europe to the Pacific Ocean, it encompassed roughly one-sixth of the world's total land. Of course, much of this land was unusable — very few Russians lived in the vast Siberian tundra. The majority of citizens resided within the European portion of the empire. According to an 1897 census, of the 126 million people who lived in the Russian empire, 92 million of them lived in Europe.[4]

A country of peasants

Tsar Nicholas II and his family spent most of their time in the royal palace in St. Petersburg, a port city along the Baltic Sea. But most Russian citizens were not royalty like Nicholas. In fact, most people didn't even live in cities. In the early 1900s, 80 percent of Russians were peasants, living and working on small farms.[5]

3   Figes, 22.
4   Fitzpatrick, 16.
5   Wood, 5.

Peasant poverty

*Three peasant women in Moscow,
Russia during the early 1900s.*[6]

Many of Russia's peasants were descended from serfs. Serfs were
workers who were bound to work exclusively for their landlords.

---

6   Photo credit: Oleg Golovnev / Shutterstock.com

They did not have many legal rights and almost all serfs lived in extreme poverty. Serfdom was a common system throughout Europe during the Middle Ages, but was not abolished in Russia until 1861. Tsar Alexander II, the grandfather of Nicholas, had announced the Emancipation of the Russian Serfs, freeing 23 million people, over one-third of Russia's population at the time.

Although emancipation gave serfs more rights, it did not free them from poverty. To keep working their land, freed serfs had to pay redemption payments to the government in addition to regular taxes. However, many peasants found it difficult to make these payments. Making matters worse, Russian farming was not very efficient, as small villages had yet to adopt modern agricultural techniques. Farmers still used wooden ploughs, and most peasants slept in the same huts as their animals. Peasants also struggled with lack of fertile land, especially as the population continued to grow. Between 1887 and 1905, the amount of land available to each household declined by 20 percent.[7] For Russian peasants, the cycle of hunger and poverty seemed like it would never end.

 Fast Fact: According to one survey in the 1880s, two-thirds of peasant households in the central Russian province of Tambov could not even feed themselves without going into debt.[8]

---

7   Ascher, 6.
8   Figes, 104.

Politics in the countryside

While Emancipation meant peasant farmers were Russian citizens, they didn't have many of the rights typically associated with citizenship. Since Russia had a tsar, not a democratic government, peasants did not vote. Land captains, who were appointed by provincial governors, had absolute authority to fine or imprison peasants.

Although peasants technically owned their owned land, they didn't get to decide how they used it. Instead, village councils known as mirs set the rules for agricultural production. Typically, these councils would divide village fields into strips, and each household would separately farm their own strip. In many villages, mirs would sometimes redistribute strips to ensure each household had the same share.[9]

Because of Russia's large geographic area, most peasant villages remained largely isolated from Russia's central government. While government officials would occasionally stop by to collect taxes, peasants knew relatively little of city life. Historians have observed that peasants were loyal to their villages and households, rather than the Russian empire.[10] However, this disloyalty had little political implication. Because peasants were largely illiterate, they mostly stayed out of politics.

---

9   Fitzpatrick, 17.
10   Pipes, 218.

Late industrialization

The tsar and his advisors recognized that Russia was behind most European powers. They saw industrialization as a way to boost the power and greatness of the Russian empire. In 1891, Alexander III ordered the construction of the Trans-Siberian Railway to connect Russia's European cities to the Pacific Ocean. The central government financed much of Russia's industrial development. By 1900, the government owned two-thirds of Russia's mining and 70 percent of its railways.[11]

The Trans-Siberian railway, the longest railway in the world.

---

11   Ascher, 12.

The new industrial proletariat

The development of industry in Russia also led to the emergence of a new social class, known as the industrial proletariat. (The word *proletariat* refers to the working class). Members of the industrial proletariat lived in cities and worked in factories, producing goods like textiles or equipment. These new industrial workers did not necessarily face better conditions than the peasants. On average, they worked 11.5 hours per day, five days a week. Half of industrial workers still couldn't read or write.[12]

Compared to the total population of Russia, however, the industrial proletariat was fairly small. In 1914, just 3 million Russians — about two percent of the population — worked in industry.[13]

Problems for Nicholas

As Russia entered the twentieth century, Tsar Nicholas II was soon to encounter several major problems. On the international scene, Russia became embroiled in a conflict with Japan that would be both embarrassing and expensive. At home, growing anger at the tsar's policies led to massive protests. The tsar wasn't prepared for either challenge.

---

12   Ascher, 14.
13   Fitzpatrick, 20.

The Japanese embarrassment

Japan, like Russia, developed slower than most major powers. However, Japan's restoration of imperial rule in 1868 led to massive industrialization. By the early 1900s, Japan looked like a major world power. Still, the major European powers did not view Japan as an equal — partially because it occupied a different part of the world, and partially because its people were seen as racially inferior. When conflict arose between Japan and Russia in 1904, Nicholas thought he would have an easy victory. He was very wrong.

From timber to war

In 1902, a Russian businessman named A. M. Bezobrazov set up a timber company in eastern Russia. When the Korean government granted him permission to cut timber on the Yalu and Tumen rivers, Japan began to get nervous, viewing Bezobrazov's timber business as an encroachment into their sphere of influence. The Japanese government proposed an agreement, which would allow Russia to expand into the Manchuria region of China, while Japan could have Korea. Nicholas didn't see the Japan question as important and didn't respond immediately.

To the tsar's shock, Japan launched a surprise attack at the Russian naval base of Port Arthur in February 1904. Japanese torpedoes struck several Russian ships, causing substantial damage. Suddenly, Japan and Russia were at war. Still, the tsar and his advisors viewed the conflict with Japan as a minor inconvenience that would quickly end in Russian victory.

Loss after loss

Russia faced several major issues from the outset of the conflict. Russian kept most of its army and navy in the European portion of the country, over four thousand miles from the battle. The Trans-Siberian Railway was still underdeveloped — it only had one set of tracks — making it difficult for the Russian military to get reinforcements.

Russia's military strategy only made things worse. Russian infantrymen only had bayonets, yet the Russian High Command repeatedly ordered them to charge at Japanese artillery. These repeated charges made it easy for Japan to fire down onto the Russian soldiers, killing a lot of people.

The tsar and his advisors also underestimated Japan's naval strength. Port Arthur fell to Japan in January 1905. In May of that same year, the Japanese and Russian navies engaged in battle at the Straits of Tsushima. Within forty-five minutes, the Japanese destroyed 21 Russian ships and captured six others. Japan, not Russia, was the master of the North Pacific.

The embarrassing naval defeat made Nicholas realize that Russia needed to make peace. In September 1905, Japan and Russia signed a peace deal, granting Japan control over Korea and much of South Manchuria.

Militarily, the Russo-Japanese was a significant setback for Russia. Economically, the war had interrupted the production of goods like cotton, hurting the livelihoods of many rural peasants. Politically, the loss was humiliating for Russia on the stage of European politics. But for Tsar Nicholas II, the war was not even the biggest challenge of 1905.

Fast Fact: The Treaty of Portsmouth, which officially ended the Russo-Japanese War, was signed at the Portsmouth Navy Yard in Kittery, Maine, in the United States. American president Theodore Roosevelt won a Noble Peace Prize for mediating negotiations between Russia and Japan.

The revolution of 1905

In the fall of 1904, groups of educated liberals, many of whom were unhappy with the tsar's involvement in Japan, began a banquet campaign. At these banquets, or meetings — which were officially to celebrate the fortieth anniversary of judicial reforms implemented under Alexander II — they called for political reforms and a constitution.

The imperial government opposed the meetings, but decided to allow them to happen. However, when the attendees proposed political reforms, Nicholas was not interested. His refusal to even consider basic reforms frustrated his opposition.

Educated liberals were not the only group critical of the tsar. Labor unrest had been growing in both the countryside and the cities. Between 1894 and 1904, there were an average of 176 strikes per year.[14] Farmers and industrial workers, who had long

---

14   Ascher, 15.

endured difficult conditions, began to direct their anger at the tsar.

Bloody Sunday

Father Georgii Apollonovich Gapon was a Russian Orthodox priest and labor organizer. A talented public speaker, he founded the Assembly of Russian Factory and Mill Workers of St. Petersburg in 1903. Gapon was not calling for revolution. His group mostly avoided political action. He claimed his goal was to help industrial workers gain better conditions while also securing their loyalty to the tsar. While Russia's most radical activists did not trust him, he gained an impressive following of everyday laborers.

In January 1905, workers at one factory in St. Petersburg went on strike to protest the firing of several of their colleagues. Gapon endorsed the strike and planned a rally that following Sunday, January 9, when he and his followers would present a list of demands to the tsar. These demands included an elected assembly, the right to establish unions, and an eight-hour working day. They did not call for Nicholas to step down.

The tsar's administration worried that Gapon's rally would bring violence. On January 7, the government ordered Gapon to call off the rally, but he refused. The government then announced that protesters would not be allowed to present their demands to the tsar and would be barred from the city's center, where the imperial palace was located. Additionally, the government called in over 12,000 troops in anticipation of clashes.[15]

15   Ascher, 27.

That Sunday, the ground in St. Petersburg was covered in snow. Church bells rang in the early morning as 150,000 workers and their families marched through the city.[16] Ignoring the government's orders, they headed straight for the city's center. When they reached the Narva Gates, which separated the imperial palace from the rest of the city, they encountered a unit of Russian infantrymen. Some protestors scattered, but others continued to advance. The soldiers fired two warning shots into the air. Then, lowering their rifles, they aimed their third shot directly into the crowd of marchers.

People screamed and fell to the ground, but the soldiers continued firing. Chaos ensued as marchers ran in every direction. Gapon was knocked to the ground but managed to escape. As the survivors spread out across the city, bringing with them news of

16   Figes, 173.

their struggle, clashes broke out between soldiers and protestors in other places. That afternoon, a group of survivors, numbering roughly 60,000 people, made one last attempt to reach the royal palace. When they arrived, they were greeted by cannons and soldiers mounted on horseback. Anticipating trouble, many protesters sunk to their knees, but the soldiers fired into the crowd once again.

The days following the massacre were filled with confusion and questions. Who ordered the soldiers to fire on unarmed protestors? The answer is unclear. Regardless, by the end of the day, about 200 people were dead, and another 800 were injured.[17] January 9, which came to be known as Bloody Sunday, marked the beginning of Russia's 1905 revolution.

Fast Fact: Gapon, fearing for his life after the events of Bloody Sunday, cut his hair and his beard and left for Switzerland a few weeks later.[18]

Rebellion

Outrage over the events of Bloody Sunday soon turned into a sense of rebellion that spread far beyond St. Petersburg. Students at Moscow University burned a picture of the tsar. In the countryside, peasants began organizing strikes to force their landowners to increase wages. When that summer brought a bad harvest, some peasants attacked landowners' estates, seizing property and setting fire to the manors. Most of the peasant

17   Figes, 178.
18   Figes, 178.

violence occurred in Russia's central agricultural zone, where poverty was the worst.

The government wasn't going to stand for peasant rebellion. Between January and October of 1905, the tsar's administration authorized over 2,700 uses of military troops against peasant uprisings.[19] Because many soldiers were from peasant families, some sympathized more with the rebels than with the regime. In June, soldiers in part of the Black Sea Fleet revolted against their commanders. The ensuing conflict killed over 2,000 people.[20]

Nicholas responds

Characteristically, Tsar Nicholas II was slow to respond to the unrest. Initially, he seemed in denial about the severity of the problem. He blamed foreign infiltrators for the Bloody Sunday demonstrations, believing that his people remained loyal to him.

Finally admitting he had a problem, Nicholas issued an Imperial Manifesto and Decree on February 18. The statement condemned the disorder but asked anyone with ideas for improvement to send them to the tsar directly. In the following weeks, village assemblies, army regiments, and other groups sent Nicholas tens of thousands of letters.

The tsar's critics, however, were skeptical of his commitment. Indeed, the February decree did not stop the rebellion. Peasant and workers' movements became more organized as the year

19   Figes, 184.
20   Figes, 184.

continued. In October, railway workers decided to strike; their strike soon spread to other industries. Within two weeks, over two million workers — across professions like factory workers, pharmacists, actors, bankers, and telegraph operators — had left their jobs. Deprived of basic economic services, the Russian empire was effectively paralyzed.

Nicholas had to do something about the October strike. If he deployed the military, he risked a massacre far worse than Bloody Sunday. Instead, on October 17, he released another document. The Manifesto on the Improvement of the State Order, more commonly known as the October Manifesto, was a victory for protestors. It granted fundamental civil freedoms, including freedom of speech and assembly. And it established the Duma, a democratically elected body whose approval would be required for new laws.

Once again, masses gathered in the streets. But this time it was for celebration, not protest. The tsar's concessions had appeased the protestors for now. The 1905 conflict was over, but the revolutionary spirit had not left Russia.

Chapter 2: The Great War

On June 28, 1914, several shots rang out on a street corner in the city of Sarajevo, located in Bosnia, a territory belonging to the Austro-Hungarian Empire. The shooter was a 19-year-old Bosnian man named Gavrilo Princip. The victims were Archduke Franz Ferdinand, heir to the Austro-Hungarian throne, and his wife Sophie, the Duchess of Hohenberg.

Princip's murder plot, though successful, was full of strange coincidences. Earlier in the day, a friend of his, Nedeljko Cabrinovic, had thrown a bomb at the car carrying the archduke and duchess. The bomb hit the back of the car and exploded. A few officers were injured, but the royal couple had survived unscathed.

A few hours later, Ferdinand and Sophie were on their way to visit the injured officers in the hospital when their driver took a wrong turn. He realized his mistake and began to back up and turn around. Coincidentally, Princip just happened to be standing on the very street corner where the open car carrying the archduke and duchess was pulling a U-turn. Seeing his chance, he fired into the open car, killing both the archduke and his wife. Soon, the Bosnian teenager would have provoked one of the worst conflicts in human history.

Nedeljko Cabrinovic (second from right, 1895-1916), attempted assassin of Archduke Franz Ferdinand (1863-1914) and Duchess Sophie Chotek (1868-1914).

The assassination of Archduke Franz Ferdinand might seem to have little to do with Russia. However, Austria-Hungary quickly sought revenge for the archduke's death. In the resulting strife, a complex system of alliances drew Russia — and many other countries — into the First World War. The war would ultimately kill 17 million people across Europe. In Russia, it would also inspire a revolution.

Fast Fact: When Gavrilo Princip was interrogated by Austro-Hungarian authorities shortly after the shooting, he said he was sorry for killing the Duchess. He had only intended to assassinate Franz Ferdinand.[1]

Why War?

Princip's assassination of Franz Ferdinand was not random. Austria-Hungary had annexed Bosnia, Princip's home country, in 1908. Princip and his friends were Serbian nationalists; they wanted Bosnia to be part of the neighboring country of Serbia instead. Princip didn't have a grudge against the archduke, but he figured that assassinating a prominent Austro-Hungarian official would send a message.

Given Princip's political motivation, the Austro-Hungarian Empire blamed Serbia for the assassination. After consulting with its close ally Germany, Austria-Hungary issued a long list of demands for Serbia known as the July Ultimatum. Among other things, the July Ultimatum demanded that Serbia arrest several of its own military and civil leaders, condemn any anti-Austro-Hungarian propaganda, and bring in the Austro-Hungarian police to help suppress further Serbian nationalist movements. If Serbia didn't comply with the terms of the ultimatum, Austria-Hungary threatened war.

---

1   Dedijer, 579.

Serbia didn't want to go to war, but it didn't want to meet these demands either. In an attempt to avoid conflict, the Serbian government sought help from other European countries and asked Austria-Hungary to negotiate. But Austria-Hungary was not in the mood for negotiations.

War was approaching.

Alliances

In 1914, the Austro-Hungarian Empire was considerably more powerful than Serbia. Yet neither country was preparing for war alone. Both countries had allies, and these allies would soon become part of the conflict.

Russia and Serbia

Russia was Serbia's biggest ally. The alliance was not particularly strategic, but instead was based on shared ethnicity. The people of both Russia and Serbia were Slavic. Deep historical rivalries created tension between Slavic people (like the Serbs and Russians) and Germanic people (like Germans and Austrians). Many Russians saw the July Ultimatum as an attack on their own dignity. Russia could not sit still while Austria-Hungary humiliated her "little Slav brother."

Tsar Nicholas II was initially reluctant to go to war. He knew that fighting a war would be difficult. The Russian military had not fully recovered from its defeat to Japan; military experts said it wouldn't be prepared for war until 1917.[2] Still, Nicholas was sympathetic to the Serbian cause. Public opinion in Russia further swayed the tsar in favor of war. Russian citizens remembered the humiliation of losing to Japan and saw another war as a way to redeem their country. Under pressure from the Duma and the press, Nicholas assured Serbia of his support.

The rest of Europe

Austria-Hungary officially declared war on Serbia on July 28, 1914, exactly one month after the assassination of Archduke Franz Ferdinand. Since Russia had promised to defend Serbia, Nicholas called for a partial mobilization of Russian troops. A few days later, when it became clear that partial troops weren't enough, the tsar ordered a full mobilization.

Russia and Serbia weren't the only countries to form an alliance. Prior to issuing the July ultimatum, Austria-Hungary had received an assurance of support from Germany. So, Germany declared war on Russia on August 1. That same day, Germany also signed a treaty with the Ottoman Empire. Meanwhile, France (which was allied with Russia) mobilized its army on behalf of Russia against Germany.

The alliance between Russia and France meant Germany would have to fight a war in both its eastern and western fronts. Knowing that a two front war would be difficult, German military strategists decided to strike first by attacking France. Though France and Germany share a border, the German

2   Figes, 249.

military decided to invade France by going through Luxembourg and Belgium. This action brought Britain, an ally of Belgium, into the fray. By the end of the month, Japan and Montenegro also declared war on Germany. The conflict between Austria-Hungary and Serbia had turned into a world war.

Players in the First World War, 1914

Central Powers	Allies
Germany	Russia
Austria-Hungary	Serbia
Ottoman Empire	Britain
	France
	Japan
	Montenegro

Fast Fact: Tsar Nicholas II and Kaiser Wilhelm II of Germany were third cousins. (The Kaiser was also the first cousin of the tsarina Alexandra). As war approached, they sent each other increasingly desperate telegrams, signed informally with their nicknames "Nicky" and "Willy."

War and Politics

On August 26, just a few weeks after Germany had declared war on Russia, German troops ambushed Russian soldiers in the forests near the city of Tannenberg. The battle lasted four days; for Russia, it ended in humiliating defeat. In total, 70,000 Russian soldiers were killed and another 100,000 were captured as prisoners. Though Tannenberg was just one battle, the optimism that many in Russia had initially felt about the war was fading quickly.

Russian prisoners of war (POWs) include Tartar and Kyrgyz prisoners. 1914-15. In the course of the war, over 4 million Russians became POWs on the Eastern Front. An estimated 90% survived to be released.

Russia at war

Following the Battle of Tannenberg, Russia did make some military advances, but many of these victories were wiped out by a German counteroffensive in May of 1915. As the war continued, it was clear that Russia was facing several major problems.

Russia's weaknesses

It was clear from the beginning of the war that Russia lacked strong military leadership. The army's top commanders were largely aristocrats with little military experience. In fact, the Grand Duke Nikolai, the Supreme Commander of the Russian forces, had never taken part in any serious battle prior to the war.

Tsar Nicholas II seemed to appoint generals based on personal relationships rather than military skill. In the spring of 1915, he visited part of the Russian army under the command of Aleksei Brusilov in Galicia, part of modern-day Poland. Afterwards, he appointed Brusilov as a General-Adjutant, a serious promotion. Nicholas admitted, however, that the appointment was not due to Brusilov's skill as a commander, but simply because the pair had enjoyed lunch together.[3]

Lack of transportation and communication was another serious problem for Russia. When the war began, Russia only had 679 cars (and two ambulances) for its entire army![4] Furthermore, Russia's railroad system was inadequate. While Germany could shuttle soldiers quickly from one place to another depending on where they were needed, Russia's military trains could not travel more than 200 miles in a day. Since space on trains was limited, Russia primarily used its railroads to transport goods and horses, while soldiers sometimes had to walk.

---

3   Figes, 260.
4   Figes, 261.

Russian men and women railroad track workers on the job in Petrograd, 1922. The Bolsheviks promoted the ideal of women's equality, a novel idea at the time, and one that was imperfectly implemented.

The Russian army had some telephone and morse-coding machines, but these frequently broke down. As a result, commanders frequently had to move around on horseback to figure out what was going on.

Lots of men

Russia did have one major advantage over its foes — it had a lot of soldiers. The population of Russia in 1914 was greater than that of Germany and Austria-Hungary combined. Russian military commanders felt that their army could afford to lose many men because a new supply was sure to arrive soon. Nonetheless, the causalities eventually added up. By 1917, 37 percent of Russian working-age men had been drafted into the army.

At times, Russia had more men than equipment. When this happened, soldiers were sent to battle without weapons. These unarmed men would wait until one of their fellow soldiers died, and then pick up a rifle from his body.

 Fast Fact: In 1914, Russia lost 1.8 million soldiers in battle, even though the war didn't start until August.[5]

Nicholas the military commander

In July 1915, Germany launched an offensive toward the Russian cities of Riga and Vilnius. Russia's defense strategy relied on a series of heavily armed fortresses. But when faced with Germany artillery assaults, these fortresses turned out to be useless. As the Germans advanced, they fired round after round, forcing Russian soldiers to retreat. Because the army had concentrated all its resources and ammunition in just a few fortresses, retreating soldiers were left with nothing.

Facing a shameful retreat, the Russian High Command hoped to implement scorched-earth tactics to trap the German army. A century earlier, the Russian army in retreat from Napoleon

5   Figes. 257.

had burned farms and towns behind them, leaving the French emperor with no resources in the harsh Russian winter. Napoleon's army had experienced mass starvation and had been forced to retreat. This time, however, the strategy didn't go as well. Confused and panicking, Russian troops randomly destroyed towns and farms. The Russian citizens who had lived in the region saw their livelihoods destroyed by their own army.

In a letter, one Russian soldier described the scene: "You can see children crying, and in some instances parents lose their children, and everywhere you hear the weeping and wailing of the poor Poles, because they are being moved out, and their grain and houses are being burned, so as to leave nothing to the Germans."[6]

Fast Fact: The Russian capital city, St. Petersburg, was renamed Petrograd in 1914 after Germany declared war on Russia. "Burg" comes from the German word for city, and patriotic Russians didn't want their capital city to be associated with their enemy.

From his palace in Petrograd, Nicholas heard news of Russia's defeats. Distraught at his country's destruction, he made a fateful decision: he decided to take command of the army himself.

Who's in charge?

To command the army, Nicholas left his home in Petrograd for the city of Mogilev, which housed Russia's military headquarters.

6   Daly and Trofminov, 12.

Nicholas thought that commanding the army would be an assertion of his authority. In the imperial capital, however, his absence created uncertainty about who was in charge.

The Duma, the legislative council established after the 1905 revolution, didn't seem to provide direction. To show patriotism and faith in the tsar, the Duma had suspended itself following Russia's declaration of war in 1914. Though the Duma was summoned and dissolved several times in the following years, it had relatively little impact on Russia's military policies. However, as the war progressed and conditions in Russia worsened, members of the Duma became increasingly critical of the tsar's regime.

The influence of Rasputin

Nicholas' absence in the royal court also opened up room for Rasputin, the tsarina's suspicious advisor. With her husband gone, Alexandra increasingly relied on Rasputin, taking his advice on a variety of policy matters.

Most members of the Russian aristocracy, however, didn't share the tsarina's love for Rasputin. While Alexandra believed he had mystical powers, most people viewed him as a quack. Many aristocrats found his behavior embarrassing, and he was accused of sexual deviancy on multiple occasions. To people familiar with the royal family, the fact that Rasputin had any influence at all was evidence of the tsar's incompetence.

In December 1916, a group of aristocrats, led by Prince Felix Yusupov, plotted to murder Rasputin. They invited the controversial figure to a banquet, where they laced his food and wine with poison. Somehow, the poison didn't affect Rasputin, so Yusupov grabbed his revolver and shot Rasputin in the chest.

"The bullet had passed through the region of the heart," Yusupov later recalled. "There could be no doubt about it; he was dead."[7]

A few minutes later, however, Rasputin woke up. Despite the bullet wound in his body, he managed to struggle to his feet and walk out Yusupov's door. Realizing the situation, one of Yusupov's guests followed Rasputin into the courtyard and shot him again. To avoid any risk of Rasputin's survival, several guests wrapped his body in a blanket and threw it into the Nevka River.

To this day, Rasputin's resistance to death has added to his mystical status. The exact events that took place at Yusupov's palace are disputed; some historians consider Yusupov's testimony unreliable. Nonetheless, Rasputin's death is certain: a few days after the banquet, local police pulled his body from the river.

The War for Ordinary Russians

While the First World War caused power struggles and drama among Russia's aristocrats, it brought more serious problems for tens of millions of the empire's peasants. As conditions worsened

---
7   Daly and Trofminov, 29.

and news trickled in of Russia's military struggles, many Russian citizens began directing their anger at the man in charge: Tsar Nicholas II.

Things start going downhill

The war seriously disrupted nearly all aspects of Russia's economy. High casualty numbers led Russia to draft more soldiers into the army. Many of these soldiers had previously been peasant farmers; after they left, their farms went untended, hurting production. As the war continued, Russia not only lost workers, but also lost valuable farmland. German attacks in Eastern Europe forced Russia to cede, or surrender, territory; therefore, Russia lost the ability to grow crops on this land.

Making matters worse, the war damaged or interfered with most of Russia's railway system. As a result, it became difficult to transport food from the countryside to the city. The loss of workers, the difficulties of transportation, and the decline in supply of vital goods like food led to inflation, a substantial increase in prices of nearly all goods in the Russian economy.

"After such an escalation of prices, what is left to eat for the poor folk?" one Russian newspaper asked.[8]

Food shortages

Indeed, Russia seemed to be running out of food. In cities like Petrograd and Moscow, women and children lined up for hours

8   Daly and Trofminov, 24.

hoping to buy a partial loaf of bread. Refugees from territory conquered by Germany — having nowhere else to go — flowed into Russia's major cities. These hordes of disoriented farmers and their families were met only with hunger and misery.

In 1916, the Russian government attempted to address concerns about shortages by introducing rationing. However, the rationing plan was chaotic, and many shopkeepers ignored it entirely.

Food shortages also reached the Russian military. Even fighting soldiers didn't always get the meals the needed. Unsurprisingly, hungry soldiers quickly grew disillusioned with the war. Some cut off their fingers or toes so they would be discharged and others deserted or even turned themselves in to the enemy, preferring to be German prisoners-of-war than to fight for their country.

Strikes

In 1914, Russian workers were too loyal to strike. The surge of patriotism at the beginning of the war meant that many factory workers saw their jobs as essential to their empire's victory. However, when Russia wasn't winning and conditions in cities were deteriorating, workers began walking out in protest. Since Russia was already facing labor shortages due to the war, these mass strikes meant that major cities essentially stopped functioning.

Хлѣба! Защитникамъ земли, взятой крестьяна- ми у помѣщиковъ.

Для успѣшной борьбы с надвигающеюся опасностью нѣмецкаго рабства и буржуазной кабалы необходимо весь сѣверъ Россіи НЕМЕДЛЕННО обезпечить хлѣбомъ!

Хлѣба! борцамъ за власть Крестьянъ, рабочихъ и солдатъ.

Ко всему крестьянству хлѣбородныхъ областей и губерній

БРАТЬЯ КРЕСТЬЯНЕ!

Дорогіе братья! Крикомъ души мы, боевые революціонеры обращаемся к Вамъ съ этимъ призывомъ.

о закрѣпленіи передачи трудящимся земли безъ выкупа, фабрики, заводовъ и банковъ.

Шлите намъ хлѣба, чтобы мы не были измучены голодомъ и имѣли бы возможность крѣпко держать в своихъ рукахъ винтовку про- тивъ разбойниковъ міра.

СОЦИАЛИСТИЧЕСКОЕ ОТЕЧЕСТВО ВЪ ОПАСНОСТИ!

Хлѣба! Хлѣба! Хлѣба!

Ссыпайте хлѣбъ в пустующіе элеваторы, в амбары и ссыпные пункты баз станцій желѣзныхъ дорогъ и пристаней су- доходныхъ рѣкъ.

Хлѣба! Хлѣба! Хлѣба! Хлѣба!

Bread! For the defenders of the peasants' land taken from the landlord.

To win the fight against the threatening danger of German slavery and bourgeois serfdom it is necessary to supply IMMEDIATELY all northern Russia with bread.

Bread! To the fighters for the power of the peasant, worker and soldier.

To the peasants of all the bread-producing districts and provinces

BROTHER PEASANTS!

Dear brothers! From the depths of our souls we, fighting revolutionists, appeal to you. ANSWER THE CALL! The last hour of the decisive battle strikes. This is the question at stake.

LAND TO THE TOILERS WITHOUT COMPENSATION, THE FACTORIES, SHOPS AND BANKS.

Send us bread, that we may not be broken by hunger and that we may be able to hold up our bayonets against the cut-throats of the world.

THE SOCIALISTS FATHERLAND IS IN DANGER!

Bread! Bread! Bread!

Bring your bread to the empty elevators and granaries, to the shipping-points on railways and the wharves of navigable rivers.

Our railroads have broken down on account of unprecedented disorders. Cowards, marauders and speculators having put on soldiers' uniforms are doing violence at the railway stations and are thus hindering the regular movement of trains.

True and class-conscious soldiers, peasants and workers of the Revolution! We appeal to you to aid those guarding our railways, and to stop the hooligans from further violence. All these destroyers of the railways are helping our bitter enemy—the German bourgeoise, and are therefore—without the law.

Bread! Bread! Bread! Bread!

(This is the translation of the Russian text on opposite page.)

The Bolshevik notice to peasants of all the bread producing districts. 1918-20. It reads, "Public order: To the peasants of all the bread producing districts and provinces; BREAD! BREAD! BREAD!"

Meeting in the Putilov Works in Petrograd during the 1917 Russian Revolution. In February 1917, strikes at the factory contributed to the February Revolution.

In 1915, there were over 1,000 industrial strikes in Russia involving half a million workers. In June of that year, a group of female textile workers went on strike to protest food shortages. In a public proclamation, they explained their motives: "They say: work calmly, but we are hungry and we cannot work. We asked but were not heard; we began to demand, and they shot at us. They say there is no bread. Where is it then?"[9]

The number of workers involved in strikes increased in 1916, and on the anniversary of Bloody Sunday in January 1917, over 140,000 workers went on strike, shutting down half the factories in Petrograd.

9   Daly and Trofminov, 11.

It's the tsar's fault!

While workers in the imperial capital were striking, Nicholas was hundreds of miles south, commanding the military from its headquarters in Mogilev. In his absence, he became an easy target for the struggles of his empire. Popular sentiment in Russia was steadily building against the tsar.

Military defeats

Nicholas assumed the position of military commander thinking that he could turn around Russia's string of defeats. However, he was not particularly equipped for the position: he lacked military experience himself, played favorites, and valued perceived loyalty of his generals over skill.

Given Nicholas's weaknesses, it's not surprising that his presence as military commander did not substantially improve Russia's outcomes. Although Russia won a few battles in 1916, the war showed no sign of ending. Since Nicholas was in charge, Russian citizens could now blame him for the empire's military losses.

Suspicion of Alexandra

When Nicholas left Petrograd, his wife, the tsarina Alexandra, began to exert more power. However, Alexandra wasn't popular with the Russian aristocrats or the public. In particular, her German roots led to accusations of disloyalty or even treason. Russians fighting against Germany wondered if they ought to be fighting against the imperial regime, too.

*National militia firing on a Tzarist police position
during the Russian Revolution, 1917.*

Alexandra was not actually a traitor, but she wasn't a particularly effective tsarina, either. As the war carried on, she seemed cold and aloof to the struggles of Russian citizens. Like her husband, she believed her own decisions were always correct, and she typically refused to listen to advisors. She was distraught following Rasputin's death and convinced Nicholas — despite the urging of other advisors — to seriously punish his murderers. In fact, the death of Rasputin, perhaps the least popular man in the empire, only pushed Nicholas closer to Alexandra, one of its least popular women. The tsar himself was losing approval fast. It was only a matter of time before tensions erupted.

Chapter 3: Revolutionary Ideas

"We lost faith in the ability of this Government to achieve victory!"[1] declared a Russian man named Paval Miliukov in a speech on November 1, 1916. His proclamation was met with cries of "it's true!" from the crowd.

Ironically, Miliukov himself was a member of the government. He had been elected to the Duma as a member of the Constitutional Democrat party. Yet many members of the Duma, like peasants, workers, and soldiers across the country were wondering how much longer the tsar's regime could continue.

Even as opposition to Tsar Nicholas II grew, his opponents were divided on who ought to take his place and govern the empire. Conservatives hoped Nicholas might abdicate and be replaced with another monarch. Certain military commanders thought they might be able to seize power. Liberals in the Duma hoped to bring democracy to Russia. A growing group of revolutionaries wanted to make Russia the world's first socialist state.

---

1   Daly and Trofminov, 25.

Duma messengers protected by Armed guards during the Russian Revolution in 1917.

Marxism in Russia

Karl Marx was a German-born writer and philosopher. He died in 1883, long before the outbreak of Russian Revolution. Yet Marx's influence lived on long after his death. His most significant work was a pamphlet titled "The Communist Manifesto," which outlined his thoughts on workers, social class, and economic systems. Many of Russia's revolutionary leaders were strongly impacted by Marx's ideas.

Fast Fact: Marx ended The Communist Manifesto with the sentence: "Working Men of All Countries, Unite!"

Marx's ideas

Marx believed that all social and political relations were based on a fundamental battle between the proletariat (the working class) and the bourgeoisie, the upper class who controlled the means of production in an economy. The means of production referred to physical things that are used to produce goods or services. For example, the fields that grow crops or the factories that produce tools are part of the means of production.

Class struggle

According to Marx, all societies were built on one social class having power over another. Under capitalism, the prevailing economic system in the 1800s, Marx argued that the bourgeoisie kept power over the proletariat by forcing workers to sell their labor. This control resulted in the commodification of workers — the valuing of people only for the economic production they created.

Marx saw the wealthy bourgeoisie as a new kind of autocrat. Although much of the industrialized world was moving toward democracy, Marx said that political freedom was irrelevant without economic freedom. Members of the proletariat — regardless of where they lived — did not have this economic freedom.

Marx thought that small changes were not enough to resolve the problems of capitalism. He believed that only a revolution could overthrow the capitalist system and replace it with communism, an economic system where there is no social class and the workers control the means of production. Marx said that the tension between the proletariat and the bourgeoisie made a communist revolution inevitable.

For a revolution to be possible, Marx believed that the proletariat had to achieve something called class consciousness. Essentially, workers had to see that they were a part of a system much bigger than themselves. Therefore, Marx thought that his communist revolution would happen in industrialized countries first. A poor farmer who worked in a rural village would not have class consciousness. But a factory worker who didn't make much despite working overtime on the factory floor with hundreds of other men might begin to feel united with his fellow workers.

Fast Fact: The words "communism" and "socialism" are often used interchangeably, but they have slightly different meanings. Socialism means that all people contribute to the production of goods and that those goods are shared equally. Communism, which Marx considered to be a later version of socialism, implies that the workers (as a whole) also have control on how those goods are produced.

Applying Marxist theory to Russia

Marx speculated that countries like Germany and France, which had already experienced massive industrialization, would see communist revolutions in the nineteenth century. They didn't

— when the First World War erupted in 1914, no country had experienced the communist revolution that Marx thought would happen.

Russia was not as developed as Germany or France — its society was still largely agricultural, not industrial. During his lifetime, even Marx was skeptical of Russia's chances of achieving a communist revolution. Marx repeatedly stated that his critique of capitalism and the call for revolution only applied to Western Europe; he considered Russia to be "an Asiatic society."[2]

Marx didn't live to see Russia's industrialization, but while Russia did see industrial growth prior to the revolution, Marxist theory still didn't explain the country's internal strife. Although Russian workers did engage in labor strikes during the First World War, their anger was primarily directed at the tsar. Russia's conflict was not the proletariat versus the bourgeoisie. Instead, it was a conflict between the tsar and his opponents, which included workers, aristocrats, peasants, and some members of the bourgeoisie.

Marxism in Russia

Even if Russia wasn't ready for a Marxist revolution, there were people in Russia who believed that such a revolution was necessary. The first Russian Marxist group was founded in 1883 — the same year Marx died — by four Russians living in Switzerland. The group — made up of George Plekhanov, Paul Axelrod, Leo Deutsch and Vera Zasulich — initially thought that

---

2   Wittfogel, 491.

Russia could forage its own path toward socialism.[3] However, as Russia began to industrialize, they changed their views, believing that their country would pass through the capitalist stage to the inevitable socialist revolution as Marx described.

Early Marxism in Russian politics

In 1898, the Russian Social Democratic Labor Party (RSDRP) held its first Congress, or meeting. Leaders of the Congress hoped that it would unite people with similar ideas into one revolutionary Marxist party. Unfortunately, only nine people showed up to the Congress, and its organizers were quickly imprisoned for inciting rebellion against the tsar.

The RSDRP wasn't the only Russian political party with Marxist influences. A group of Russians advocating social revolution and land redistribution founded the Social-Revolutionaries (SR) Party in 1900. The SR party believed in violence as a tool to achieve political goals and carried out assassinations of several prominent Russian officials in the early 1900s.

Bolsheviks and Mensheviks

Vladimir Lenin was born in 1870 under the name Vladimir Ilyich Ulyanov. A devout Marxist, he was arrested in 1895 due to his political activities and was sentenced to exile in Siberia. Following his release in 1900, he traveled around Europe, meeting with various Marxist leaders, and he did a bit of writing. His most famous work was a pamphlet he wrote in 1902 titled

---

3   Wood, 26.

"What is to be done?" Lenin argued that it was silly to expect workers to suddenly develop a Marxist political consciousness on their own. Instead, he said, workers needed a political party that would directly advocate for revolution.

Lenin attended the RSDRP's second Congress, which was held in London in 1903. Party leaders hoped that this second meeting would bring unity. Unfortunately, the Congress ended up creating new divides among Russia's Marxists.

At the second Congress, one major issue up for debate was the requirements for membership in the RSDRP. Julius Martov, one of the attendees, suggested that members be required to work in the direction of one of the party's organizations. Lenin, however, went a step further. He believed members should be required to work for one of the party's organizations. The word choice seemed like a small issue, but it illustrated a fundamental ideological split within the RSDRP.

Those who sided with Lenin believed in a party full of committed activists; those who sided with Martov saw the party as a group of sympathetic supporters. Lenin actually lost the vote on party membership, but he won a later vote about party structure and centralization. This victory convinced Lenin that he had a majority; he named his supporters the Bolsheviks based on the Russian word for majority. Lenin called his opponents the Mensheviks, a name that came from the Russian word for minority. The split between the Bolsheviks and Mensheviks would be permanent.

Fast Fact: It was common for revolutionaries to change their names in order to confuse the police. Lenin adopted his new last name after his exile in Siberia. Historians believe he chose it due to his admiration of the Lena River.[4]

Marxists and the revolution of 1905

The Bolsheviks and the Mensheviks both disapproved of Father Gapon's demands for the tsar in 1905. They thought Gapon was not revolutionary enough and that his small demands — such as a shorter workday and greater civil liberties — would make people feel better but would fail to bring about real change.

Despite their initial skepticism, the Bolsheviks and Mensheviks also took an important lesson away from the revolution of 1905. The strength of peasant uprisings made leaders like Lenin and Leon Trotsky believe that peasants would play a crucial role in Russia's ultimate communist revolution.[5]

Ideas and the Russian Government

Marxism was hardly the only political movement to develop in Russia in the early 1900s. A group of local politicians and high-ranking professionals founded the Union of Liberation in 1904. The Union of Liberation didn't believe in revolution, but campaigned for a constitutional democracy. After 1905, most

---

4   Ascher, 68.
5   Wittfogel, 501.

of Russia's politics took place in the empire's two main elected bodies: the Duma and the soviets.

Politics under the tsar

The Duma contained about 500 elected representatives from all classes of Russian society and all political parties. Although the tsar's powers severely limited the Duma's influence, the Duma provided a hint at the many competing political ideas in Russia prior to the revolution.

Parties in the Duma

Petrograd Soviet of Workers' and Soldiers' Deputies. March 1917. The state Duma was not under the control of the Bolsheviks in the early days of the Revolution.

The Bolsheviks, Mensheviks, and Socialist Revolutionaries decided to boycott the first Duma elections in 1905. The first Duma was made up primarily of two centrist parties (the Constitutional Democrats, whose members were called Kadets, and the Union of 17 October Party, whose members were called Octobrists) and a radical party called the Labor Group. The tsar decided that this first duma was too anti-government, and he dissolved it.

The three Marxist parties decided to participate in elections for the second Duma, and each won a number of seats. Nicholas again disliked the Duma and dismissed it only a few months later.

For the third Duma, the tsar's prime minister modified the election rules to favor landowners and wealthy aristocrats while lessening the representation of peasants and workers. As a result, the Octobrists and several more conservative parties gained many seats. Nicholas was mostly satisfied with this third Duma, although he still suspended it on occasion when he needed to get certain policies through.

The fourth and final Duma was even more conservative than the third. However, the tenure of the final Duma was marked by growing disconnect between the tsar, the rest of the government, and the people. While the Duma had never been an entirely democratic body, many Russians began to feel that neither the Duma nor the tsar reflected their interests. And, as Miliukov's speech proved, many members of the Duma no longer believed in the tsar.

The development of soviets

The word "soviet" is Russian for "council." Historically, the word was used to describe a variety of political organizations. However, it took on new meaning in 1905, when workers in St. Petersburg elected a soviet of workers to represent them. By the end of the year, soviets had popped up in many other cities. Although soviets didn't technically have any political power under the tsar's regime, they came to represent workers' interest, especially when the Duma failed to. Members of the soviet often belonged to the Mensheviks, the Bolsheviks, the Socialist Revolutionaries, or another political party.

Political repression under the tsar

Tsar Nicholas II wasn't a fan of many Russian political parties, especially those with Marxist influences. Prior to 1905, Russian citizens didn't even have basic protections like freedom of speech. The tsar's secret police — called the Okhrana — could arrest anyone suspected of political crimes and exile them to Siberia. The Okhrana had thousands of spies and informants, they intercepted people's mail, and they sometimes used torture.

Although Nicholas granted basic civil rights to his citizens after the 1905 revolution, the Okhrana continued to operate and often targeted Marxists. By 1917, the average member of the Bolshevik party had spent nearly four years in jail or exile.[6] Many revolutionaries felt that the time they spent in prison prepared them for "the struggle"—the ultimate communist revolution. As it turned out, that revolution was not far away.

6   Figes, 124.

Chapter 4: The Uprising

There were women in the street, and they were hungry.
Most of them were workers in a textile factory in Petrograd, but they'd walked out on February 23, 1917, to protest recent food shortages. Some people claimed the government was secretly withholding bread. Although this rumor was probably untrue, the idea only deepened the women's anger.

"Down with the war! Down with high prices! Down with hunger! Bread to the workers!" they chanted.[1]

That winter also happened to be the coldest Petrograd had experienced in years.[2] Shortages of fuel meant that Russian citizens were both cold and hungry. So, the female textile workers who had walked out that morning decided to throw snowballs at the men's factory across the street. Soon, the male factory workers walked outside too, joining the strike. By the afternoon, there were 100,000 workers crowding the streets in the Vyborg district of Petrograd.

1   Daly and Trofimov, 36.
2   Figes, 307.

The men and women who walked out from their factory jobs on that cold February day had no idea that they were starting a revolution. A week later, it became clear.

Russia would never be the same.

Riots in Petrograd

Russians were armed to defend Petrograd.

Strikes in Russia were common during the later years of the war. Initially, the textile workers' strike didn't seem any different. The following day, another 150,000 people turned out in the streets in protest. Many of them were armed with everyday household items — hammers, rocks, screws, or whatever else they could find. By February 25, the textile strike had turned into a general strike, as all of Petrograd's major factories stopped operation. As the protests grew, they also became more political.

"Down with the tsar!" cried the marchers.[3]

To contain the protests, the government called upon both the local police and soldiers, known as Cossacks. The Cossacks were known to be brutal fighters, having crushed political demonstrations in the past. But as it turned out, this protest was different.

From strike to uprising

On the afternoon of February 25, a unit of Cossacks stopped a group of marchers near Petrograd's Kazan Cathedral. The marchers were not far from the city center, where 12 years earlier, guards had fired on protestors on Bloody Sunday. The Cossacks and the protestors seemed to be in a tense standstill when a young girl emerged from the crowd. She walked toward the soldiers and, greeting them, pulled a bouquet of roses from her jacket. The Cossacks' officer accepted the roses.

The crowd breathed a sigh of relief.

The rose exchange was a victory for the protestors, although only a symbolic one. Protestors began to see the Cossacks as fellow workers or peasants who were forced to work as soldiers for a living and began referring to them as "comrade Cossacks." The incident also hinted that soldiers, assumed to be loyal, might not always side with the tsar.

---

3   Figes, 310.

Fast Fact: Prior to 1918, Russia operated on the Julian calendar, not the Gregorian calendar that most of the world used. (The Gregorian calendar is what we use today). As a result of this distinction, February 23 in Russia was actually considered March 8 in Western Europe and the United States. The dates quoted in this book are the dates that were used in Russia at the time.

The tsar's orders

Hundreds of miles south, Tsar Nicholas II was dutifully working on plans for the army when he heard news of the protests. He had visited Petrograd only a few days earlier and had returned to Russia's military headquarters in Mogilev on February 22, the day before the riots broke out. Initially, Nicholas's advisors tried to downplay the protests, not wanting to admit that events had gotten out of hand so quickly. However, as the situation in the capital deteriorated, they called on Nicholas to take action.

To this day, historians are unsure of how much Nicholas knew about the protests. Regardless, the tsar's next decision proved fateful. He ordered the military to use whatever force was necessary to put down the disturbances.

In and around Petrograd, there were plenty of soldiers to enforce the tsar's demands. Soldiers and policemen guarded major intersections. Some rode through the streets in military vehicles, and others mounted themselves high up on buildings to get a better angle.

On Sunday, February 26, the protests resumed like normal. When marchers converged around the imperial palace, however, the police and military fired on them from several different directions. Protestors fled in all directions, and clashes continued across the city. Some workers threw bricks or pieces of ice at troops who continued to fire back. By the end of the day, at least fifty people were dead.

Protestors called it Russia's second Bloody Sunday.

The soldiers revolt

The soldiers who had been ordered onto the streets that Sunday were not advanced fighting units like the Cossacks. Many of them were recent recruits — peasants from the countryside who had been drafted because of Russia's involvement in the First World War. Instead, they found themselves fighting their own people.

On Sunday night, they returned to their barracks, tired of fighting and concerned for their fellow citizens. They sympathized with the hungry protestors: "Our fathers, mothers, sisters, brothers, and brides are begging for bread," one soldier said. "Are we going to kill them?"[4] Another man claimed that his unit had killed his own mother.[5]

Soldiers were quick to protest the next day when their commanding officer ordered them back into the streets to take down the demonstrators once again. In the Pavlovsky Regiment,

4   Lilley and Guinness.
5   Figes, 313.

soldiers first yelled and complained. Their officer, overwhelmed, began walking away. Then, for some reason, he began to run. Several soldiers raised their rifles and fired into his back. He fell to the ground.

The men had shot their own commander.

There was no turning back now.

To the streets

The unit of soldiers who had revolted against their officer quickly joined the ranks of protestors in the streets of Petrograd. Some soldiers from neighboring units followed them. Not all soldiers were rebels — indeed, loyal and rebel soldiers began to fight within units. Nonetheless, the soldiers' rebellion was a serious blow to the tsar's regime.

With the help of recently defected soldiers, the protestors captured Petrograd's Arsenal, which housed over 70,000 guns, and the city's weapons factories, where they picked up another 100,000 weapons.[6] They took over the telephone exchange and several of the city's railway stations. They stormed the tsar's jails, freeing the prisoners inside.

The battle for Petrograd was hardly over. The police largely remained loyal to the tsar, and police snipers — who were more skilled with firearms than the average worker — continued to fire into crowds of protestors. Soldiers and protestors attempted

6   Figes, 315.

to hunt down police, often beating or killing them when they found them.

Collapse of the Tsar

Tauride Palace

Nicholas, still in Mogilev, received another message from his advisors, telling him of the mutiny in Petrograd. They warned him that he needed to institute reforms immediately. "Tomorrow," one advisor warned, "will be too late."[7] The tsar was still in denial. On February 27, he called for the suspension of the Duma, but took no other political action.

---

7   Ascher, 69.

At the Tauride Palace in Petrograd, the members of the Duma heard the tsar's orders. They agreed to officially suspend themselves, but they remained in the palace. If the tsar could no longer govern Russia, they thought, someone else might have to.

Nicholas returns

Realizing that his presence in the capital was now necessary, Nicholas set out to return to Petrograd by rail. He couldn't reach the capital — his train was stopped, because the protestors had taken over railways. Nicholas, with several of his army commanders, had been hoping for a counterrevolution, but it now appeared to be too late. Though there were still forces in Petrograd loyal to Nicholas, they had failed to organize. The tsar had little chance of taking back his capital.

The last tsar

Nicholas, still trapped on his train near the city of Pskov, received telegrams from several of his military commanders, all of whom recommended that he abdicate, or renounce his throne. Russia could not win the war, they argued, when the people were revolting at home. After consulting with his advisors on the train, the tsar agreed.

On the morning of March 2, several members of the Duma headed for Psov to present Nicholas with a plan for his abdication. In according with the Law of Succession — which had governed the Russian Empire for centuries — they planned for Alexei, the tsar's only son, to assume the throne.

At the time, Alexei was 12 years-old. There was no cure for his hemophilia; doctors doubted he would live into adulthood. The tsar, who cared deeply for his son, didn't want to burden Alexei with the throne. Instead, he decided to abdicate both himself and his son in favor of his younger brother, the Grand Duke Mikhail.

This action was probably illegal — the Russian laws of succession were very strict and allowed only for the throne to pass to the tsar's oldest son. Additionally, Mikhail had married a commoner years earlier, which should have barred him from becoming the tsar. In the end, it didn't really matter. Mikhail didn't want to be tsar, and — at the urging of several members of the Duma — he immediately signed an abdication agreement of his own. Over 300 years of Romanov rule in Russia had come to an end.

 Fast Fact: Nicholas wanted to move to England with his family following his abdication. British Prime Minister David Lloyd George offered the family asylum, but King George V later canceled the invitation because he worried that British people wouldn't like the presence of the former Russian monarchs.[8]

Who's in charge now?

Although most protestors were excited to hear of the tsar's resignation, the news didn't bring peace to the streets of Petrograd. The revolution against the tsar seemed at risk of dissolving into random violence: soldiers and workers, many of

8   Ascher, 70.

them drunk, continued to wander in the streets, some of them looting, smashing shop windows, and beating people up.

The revolution had happened without revolutionary leaders. Lenin — who'd been calling for a Marxist revolution in Russia — was far away in Switzerland. In the absence of clear leadership, two different groups emerged.

The Petrograd Soviet

As the fall of the tsar looked inevitable, a crowd had gathered outside Tauride Palace, looking for leaders. On February 27, several men, including the Menshevik politician Georgy Khrustalev-Nosar, the former leader of the St. Petersburg Soviet, announced the formation of the "Provisional Executive Committee of the Soviet of Workers' Deputies." They called upon workers and soldiers to hold their own elections and send representatives to the committee.

The very next day, factories and military units across the city held their elections. In total, they elected roughly 5,000 representatives to the committee, making it way too big to function properly.[9] When the committee proceeded to hold a mass meeting in one wing of the Tauride Palace, chaos ensued. The leaders of the committee hadn't established any rules or procedures. Every action was up for debate. Representatives often talked at the same time and, stationed on opposite sides of the hall, they couldn't hear each other. Plenty of unelected

9   Ascher, 70.

officials showed up, hoping to have their say. Tallying votes was impossible.

Nikolai Nikolaevich Himmer (also referred to as Sukhanov), a socialist, was at the committee's first meeting. Despite his excitement about the revolution, he recalled being frustrated by the constant interruptions and lack of order. "I remember only unimaginable hubbub, tension, hunger, and the feeling of irritation," he later wrote.[10]

Despite the chaos, representatives to the committee were not lacking in passion. To thunderous applause, they resolved to rename the group the "Petrograd Soviet of Workers' and Soldiers' Deputies," a name that would typically be shortened to the Petrograd Soviet.

The Duma

Duma leaders, still camped out in the other wing of the Tauride Palace, were reluctant to assume power. Most members of the Duma came from upper-class backgrounds; the protestors outside terrified them. They'd seen what had happened to Nicholas. If they assumed power but didn't meet the demands of the working class, then the anger and violence in the streets might suddenly be directed at them.

However, 12 Duma members decided they couldn't sit around while Russia seemed to be falling apart. They formed a committee entitled the "Temporary Committee of Duma

10   Daly and Trofimov, 46.

Members for the Restoration of Order in the Capital and the Establishment of Relations with Individuals and Institutions." The committee's intentions were initially simple. They were not a governing body; they were a group of Duma members to help restore order to Petrograd. As they saw the power of the Soviet grow, and it became clear the tsar was truly gone, the committee began to take a more forceful tone. On March 3, they declared the formation of a provisional government, headed by Prince Georgy Lvov.

For centuries, Russia had been under the rule of a tsar. In the span of just eight days, strikes and protests in one city had been enough to topple the empire's supreme leader. Now, Duma members had assumed the role of the new government. They had the task of ruling not only the capital city, but all of Russia.

Taking out the tsar had been surprisingly easy.

Governing the Russian Empire, as they would soon find out, would be much harder.

Chapter 5:
The In-Between Time

The committee formed under Duma leaders and led by Prince Lvov soon named itself Russia's Provisional Government. Provisional meant temporary or short-term; the government announced that it would rule only until September 30, 1917, when elections would be held to decide on a constitution.

The Provisional Government's initial steps seemed promising for Russia's future as a democracy. The government guaranteed freedom of speech and legalized labor unions and strikes. It granted amnesty to people imprisoned for political or religious reasons, abolished the death penalty, and promised to repeal legal restrictions based on social or religious grounds.

Still, the Provisional Government faced numerous challenges. The Petrograd Soviet — and its elected members — wanted say in shaping the new Russia, too. Additionally, Russia was still embroiled in the First World War, a conflict that showed little sign of ending. And groups on both sides of the political spectrum were closely watching the Provisional Government for weakness, hoping for a chance to seize power themselves.

Conflict for the Provisional Government

Lvov, as it turned out, was little more than a figurehead as Russia's first prime minister. Paval Miliukov, the foreign minister, and Alexander Kerensky, the minister of justice, proved to be the ones really in control of Russia's early government. Controlling the government, however, didn't mean that they controlled the people.

The Provisional Government vs. the Soviet

Kerensky, who was both a socialist and a former member of the Duma, spent much of his time as minister of justice shuttling between the Provisional Government and the Petrograd Soviet, looking for compromise. While Kerensky and the Provisional Government had the official authority, they recognized that many of the soldiers and workers were loyal to the Soviet. Therefore, they believed it was necessary to work with the Soviet and make compromises. Otherwise, they would anger the workers and soldiers — and given what had happened to the tsar, they didn't want to do that!

The division of authority between the Petrograd Soviet and the Provisional Government is often called "dual power." Although the groups communicated, they sometimes operated like two separate governments. They generally dealt with different tasks and they sometimes sent conflicting messages.

Order No. 1

The split between the Petrograd Soviet and the Provisional Government stemmed in part from an order the Soviet released on March 1, the day before the tsar abdicated. Known as "Order No. 1" (No. is an abbreviation for "Number"), the order addressed the duties and power of the military.

During the revolution, many soldiers had revolted against their commanding officers. Several parts of Order No. 1 addressed the relationship between officers and the soldiers they commanded. According to the order, soldiers no longer had to refer to their commanding officers with names like "Your Honor" or "Your Excellency" and didn't have to salute their officers when they were off-duty.

A few parts of Order No. 1 were particularly troublesome for the Provisional Government. "That in all of their political actions military units are subordinate to the Soviet of Workers' and Soldiers' Deputies," the order declared.[1] The Soviet of Workers' and Soldiers' Deputies was the early name for the Petrograd Soviet. The order, therefore, made the soldiers loyal to the Soviet. Most soldiers — believing that the Soviet represented their interests — were happy to go along.

Additionally, Order No. 1 told soldiers that — no matter what — they should not return their rifles to their commanding officers. To the Provisional Government and its followers, it seemed unnecessary for soldiers to keep their guns. The tsar

1   Daly and Trofminov, 49.

was gone; the revolution was over; the soldiers who had helped should hand in their weapons and go home to their families. By ordering the soldiers to stay in Petrograd and stay armed, the Soviet appeared to be raising its own army.

The revolution spreads

It's important to remember that the Russian Revolution happened only in the capital city, not the whole country. News spread slowly in Russia due to a lack of reliable communication — the train moved slowly and the telegraphs only worked sometimes. People who lived outside of Petrograd heard mixed reports, creating confusion and chaos.

When news of the tsar's abdication reached cities and towns across Russia, many local government officials did not know what to do. With the tsar gone, their authority to rule seemed to disappear too. Furthermore, news of the revolution prompted uprisings in many other cities. Plenty of the factors that caused the protests in Petrograd — such as hunger and anger at the war — were common across Russia.

The Provisional Government was not powerful enough to govern or even substantially influence far-reaching cities and towns. The tsar's resignation had created a power vacuum — people desperately needed someone to govern, but it wasn't immediately clear who would do the job. Local soviets, which had traditionally been workers' councils without political power, often stepped up and took power.

Fast Fact: Because so many Russian men were at war, women made up two-thirds of the workforce. As a result, women sometimes served on the early workers' councils in parts of rural Russia.[2]

What about the war?

One major source of disagreement between the Petrograd Soviet and the Provisional Government was Russia's continued involvement in the First World War. The Bolsheviks and some others socialists had opposed the war since the beginning. They viewed it as a tool for the capitalist bourgeoisie to gain wealth, while poor peasants and workers had to fight. As the war dragged on, socialists found more and more support in their efforts to end it.

Division in the Soviet

Russia's presence in the war proved to be a divisive issue in the Petrograd Soviet. The group's executive committee favored continuing the war so long as Russia's territory was under attack. But many of its members — the everyday workers and soldiers — just wanted the war to end. Many Russian workers and peasants had seen their fathers, sons, husbands and brothers go off to war. They wanted nothing more than for the troops to come home.

---

2   Ascher, 82.

The Provisional Government's goal

The Provisional Government had more ambitious goals for Russia's war efforts. A secret treaty that the tsar had signed with Russia's allies at the start of the war had promised Russia the straights of Constantinople once they achieved victory. Miliukov in particular hoped that Russia could ultimately control the straits.

Russia's allies were hoping that 1917 would be the year they ultimately defeated Germany. A double invasion — from Russia in the east and France in the west — might be enough, they thought. Most Russian commanders thought it was crazy for Russia to launch such an offensive. Furthermore, it would be difficult for the Provisional Government to persuade the Soviet, whose support (though not officially needed) would be very helpful. Still, the Provisional Government also wanted to prove to Russia's allies that it was legitimate and saw launching an attack on Germany as a way to do that.

To lead the offensive, Kerensky selected the general Aleksei Brusilov. Brusilov had been an early supporter of the revolution and was optimistic about democracy. He also believed that an offensive attack would raise the morale of Russia's troops. The soldiers, however, weren't particularly interested in attacking Germany. Many decided to desert instead — according to Russia's official government statistics, 170,000 soldiers left the army, but historians think that the actual number was even higher.

The offensive began on June 16, 1917. Initially, the attack went well: Russian troops advanced for two days, forcing the German army to retreat. On the third day, however, Germany launched a counterattack. Facing German advancement, the Russian army broke down completely. When ordered to retreat, many soldiers ran off and deserted. Others mutinied, turning their weapons on their own commanders. As they passed through towns, many looted shops and terrorized locals. And in the abandoned town of Koniukhy, soldiers discovered a large store of alcohol and got so drunk they couldn't fight.[3] By the time they had recovered, German reinforcements arrived, and the Russian troops suffered heavy losses and were forced to retreat.

Kerensky and Brusilov had hoped for a glorious Russian victory. The actual outcome had been an ugly defeat. Russia lost hundreds of thousands of soldiers and millions of square miles of territory. The Provisional Government was losing popularity fast.

Lenin Returns

When the revolution had erupted in February, Vladimir Lenin had been safely hiding away in Zurich, Switzerland. With the collapse of the tsar, he wanted to return to Russia, but geography posed a significant problem. To cross from Switzerland to Russia, he'd have to pass through Germany, Russia's current enemy. Russia's allies probably could have helped Lenin, but — seeing as Lenin was anti-war — they didn't want to.

---

3   Figes, 419.

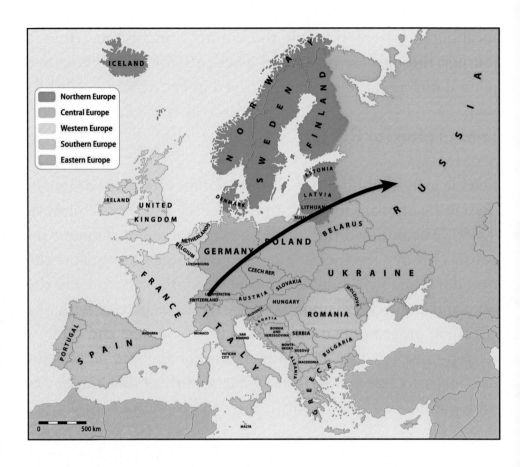

The German train

The German government, however, saw Lenin's anti-war stance as an advantage and decided to help him return to Russia. After some communication between Swiss socialists and German authorities, a train left the German town of Gottmadingen — which was just across the border from Switzerland — on March 27, carrying Lenin and 31 others.

Officially, the German government claimed that they were not involved with Lenin's return. Typically, German authorities stopped trains to check passports, but Lenin's train was sealed, meaning it passed through the country unchecked. After a journey through Germany and Sweden (which had remained neutral during the war), Lenin arrived in Petrograd on April 3.

Lenin's plan for Russia

Having arrived in his home country, Lenin wasted little time in presenting his plans for the future of Russia. In a speech on April 4, 1917, he outlined the "April Theses," a series of thoughts on Russia's future. The theses were published in the newspaper the next day. Notably, Lenin denounced Russia's involvement in the war, and even called upon soldiers to make friends with the enemy in order to obtain peace. He urged workers and soldiers to stop supporting the Provisional Government and prepare for the Soviet to take power instead. He said that, after the Soviet took power, they would redistribute land to the peasants.

Lenin's plan for Russia surprised even his political allies. Most of Russia's socialists had been tentatively allied with the Provisional Government and hoped to achieve power by winning the eventual elections; they were skeptical of Lenin's radicalism. Lenin, however, didn't give up easily. He published several essays and worked tirelessly to persuade his comrades that Russia was prepared for a communist takeover. Over the next few months, general instability and weakness from the Provisional Government seemed to indicate that Lenin was right.

The July Days

In July 1917, protests erupted again on the streets of Petrograd. Historians dispute whether the unrest simply erupted spontaneously, as it had in February, or if the Bolsheviks — Lenin's strand of socialists — helped instigate it. Regardless, the upheaval, known as the July Days, would rattle the Russian political landscape.

The unrest

Since the February Revolution, no soldiers from the capital city had been transferred to the war front. It had been one of the agreements between the Petrograd Soviet and the Provisional Government, who were still trying to work together. But the troops didn't always agree with the government, and by June, many high-ranking officials felt that the troops posed a threat to the Provisional Government. At the same time, Russia was struggling badly with the offensive, and rumors began swirling that the government would go back on its promise and send Petrograd's soldiers to war.

On July 3, a group of soldiers took to the streets with banners, calling for the Soviet to take power. Joined by workers from various factories, they marched haphazardly around the city. They lacked leaders, a direction, or a plan. But they were loud and angry. Neither the Provisional Government nor the Bolsheviks could ignore them.

Bolshevik involvement

The Bolsheviks initially had opposed an armed uprising. Lenin argued that Russia wasn't ready quite yet — the provinces outside of Petrograd needed time to warm to a socialist revolution. Otherwise, a Bolshevik takeover in the capital might lead to a civil war between the capital city and the rest of Russia.

Lenin, who was feeling ill, had actually left for Finland on June 29. He was not present in Petrograd when the riots erupted; in his absence, other Bolshevik leaders had to decide how to respond. After some debate, they agreed that it would be difficult to stop the protests, so they might as well support them. They handed out leaflets calling for organized demonstrations and a new power structure based on the Soviet, not the Provisional Government. And — feeling insecure without their leader — they sent a car to Finland to bring Lenin back.

The protests continue

On July 4, when angry workers and soldiers returned and Bolshevik leaflets flooded the streets, the mood in Petrograd turned dark. Half a million marchers took to the streets, this time with tentative Bolshevik backing. They marched to the Bolshevik headquarters, eager to see Lenin. But their leader gave them few instructions: Lenin gave a short speech calling for Soviet power, but didn't provide any instructions on how to acquire it.

Had Lenin instructed his followers to march into Tauride palace, round up members of the Provisional Government, and proclaim Soviet power, they probably would have. Instead, they continued to wander through Petrograd, clashing with police and soldiers who were loyal to the government. As they approached Tauride Palace, snipers fired into the crowd from above. Some marchers fired wildly back, although they didn't know who they were aiming at. As the crowd dispersed, the march erupted into rioting, with protestors firing into windows, looting stores, and attacking strangers in the street. Hundreds were killed.

Fast Fact: Although Lenin was known for his impassioned speeches at party meetings, he didn't particularly like giving public speeches. According to his wife, he became nervous when he had to speak to the masses.[4]

Consequences of the July Days

The Provisional Government was quick to crack down on the protests. Lenin immediately went into hiding, while several other leaders — include Leon Trotsky — were arrested. Seeing the need for change, the Provisional Government appointed Kerensky as the new prime minister on July 6. As a socialist and a former member of the Duma, Kerensky seemed like the ideal person to unite Russia once again.

In his first days in office, Kerensky made it clear that he no longer wanted the Soviet involved in government affairs. He

4   Figes, 428.

passed several laws restricting public gathering and re-instituted the death penalty. And on July 18, the Soviet was formerly expelled from Tauride Palace. Russia's experiment with dual power was over. The Provisional Government, under Kerensky, had official control.

The Bolshevik retreat

Kerensky's efforts to reduce the power of the Soviet were aided by a rise in anti-Bolshevism following the events of the July Days. In particular, several newspapers accused Lenin of being a German agent and suggested that the Germans were financing the Bolsheviks political actions.

There was some truth to these rumors. After all, Germany had orchestrated Lenin's return to Russia and had provided some money to the Bolsheviks through an agent known as Alexander Parvus.[5] Still, it stretch to say that Lenin or the Bolsheviks were German agents — they likely would have been fighting for communism in Russia without German support.

Nonetheless, these revelations caused plenty of trouble for the Bolsheviks. Fearing for his personal safety, Lenin again returned to Finland. Meanwhile, many average Russians — who suddenly doubted and feared the Bolsheviks — looked to the Provisional Government as leaders. The protests had backfired.

---

5   Ascher, 86.

The Kornilov Affair

Following the July Days, it seemed clear the left-wing influences, such as the Bolsheviks and the Soviet, posed a threat to the Provisional Government. However, the next challenge to Kerensky's government came not from these leftist forces, but from conservatives in the military.

The illusion of stability

Russia's flailing military needed discipline, and Kerensky thought he had the perfect man for the job. General Lavr Kornilov was a legend in the Russian military due to his dramatic escape from Austrian captivity in 1916. He was deeply patriotic and aimed, above all else, to return Russia's military to full strength.

Kornilov, however, had numerous flaws. He had very little understanding of Russian politics, and was not able to distinguish between the moderate socialists and the Bolsheviks. He had a coarse manner of speaking, which often offended government officials. And Kornilov didn't like input from others — he believed that he alone knew what was best for Russia's military. When he accepted the position of Supreme Commander of Russia's army, he insisted that he be given absolute authority over strategic military decisions and the appointments of future commanders.

General Lavr Kornilov, Army Chief of Staff
during the Russian Revolution.

The Moscow State Conference

After placing Kornilov in charge of the military, Kerensky sought to give legitimacy to his own government. He concluded that his major weakness was lack of democratic representation — people didn't feel like their government served them. The

Provisional Government had found it difficult to organize elections, and voting had already been postponed several times. Thus, Kerensky decided that the next-best option was to organize a conference and bring in delegates who — though not democratically elected — represented different parts of Russian society and different places on the political spectrum. He hoped that such a meeting would bring together people with different ideas and remind them that they all had the common goal of creating a better Russia.

The Moscow State Conference, held in August of 1917, brought in more than 2,000 representatives, including trade union members, landowners, soldiers, university professors, and delegates from both the Soviet and the Duma. Despite this apparent diversity, the conference still underrepresented Russia's masses — there were few peasants or everyday workers in attendance.

To make the conference seem more impressive, Kerensky called upon Kornilov to speak. But when the two men appeared together, their differences became quite apparent. As Kerensky took the podium, he received cheers from many of the moderates, while much of the hall was silent. When Kornilov went to make his speech, conservatives gave him an ovation, while those who had cheered for Kerensky were silent. It became clear that there was a serious division between Russia's military and political leadership.

Fast Fact: Kerensky's final speech at the Moscow State Conference was long and rambling. At one point, he paused to take a breath, so the delegates burst into applause, forcing him to end the speech.

Kerensky's fears and Lvov's deception

In the aftermath of the Moscow State Conference, Kerensky became increasingly fearful that someone would try to steal power from him. At that moment, a man named Vladimir Nikolayevich Lvov offered to give Kerensky advice. Lvov was not a terribly important figure: he was a former member of the Duma and had recently been dismissed from the Holy Synod, part of the Russian Orthodox Church. However, the prime minister decided to listen to him. Lvov proceeded to warn Kerensky that members of the military were planning to assassinate him, and offered to negotiate with Kornilov.

Kerensky would later say that he never instructed Lvov to talk with Kornilov. Regardless, Lvov traveled to Mogilev claiming to be a representative of Kerensky and met with Kornilov. Acknowledging that the Provisional Government was weak, Lvov offered Kornilov three proposals to make it stronger: Kerensky could assume the power of a dictator; a group of men — including Kornilov — could form a collective dictatorship; or Kornilov himself could become dictator. Lvov then asked Kornilov which option he preferred.

Kornilov told Lvov he preferred the third option, but he would also be willing to work under Kerensky if that was best. When Lvov returned to Petrograd, however, he told Kerensky that Kornilov had demanded the power of a dictator for himself and had issued an ultimatum, which called for Kerensky's resignation and the implementation of martial law — while Kornilov might have suggested similar measures, he hadn't demanded them.

For Kerensky, already paranoid, the message was clear: Kornilov must have been planning a coup. To confirm Kornilov's apparent treason, Kerensky, along with Lvov, planned to communicate with the general through a primitive telephone-like machine. But Lvov was late for the meeting, so Kerensky began the conversation alone. Pretending to be Lvov, he asked Kornilov to confirm that the message Lvov had passed on was correct, although he never indicated exactly what the message was. Then, being himself, he indicated he'd understood the message. The conversation was brief, and it's unclear whether either man understood what the other one was saying. At the end, Kornilov asked Kerensky to come to Mogilev to discuss matters further.

Kornilov believed that his recent conversations with Kerensky and Lvov were the beginning of negotiations to form a new government. He sent telegrams inviting various other people to meet with him and Kerensky — not exactly actions of an aspiring dictator.

Meanwhile in Petrograd, Kerensky met with his advisors. Presenting Kornilov's reported ultimatum (that Lvov had passed onto Kerensky) and transcripts from his conversation with Lvov earlier that night, he explained that Kornilov was launching a conspiracy to undermine him and demanded full authority in dealing with the emergency. While at least one of Kerensky's advisors suggested that the whole thing might have been a misunderstanding, Kerensky had already made up his mind. He saw himself as the leader of a free Russia, fighting valiantly against the authoritarian threat posed by Kornilov. His advisors agreed to resign, effectively making him dictator. And — before he went to bed — Kerensky sent Kornilov a telegram saying he was fired and demanding that he come straight to Petrograd.

Kornilov was confused by Kerensky's message. After all, the men had talked only hours earlier. He thought that the message might have been fake and that Kerensky's government must have been taken hostage by the Bolsheviks. Thus, he ordered an army unit headed by Aleksandr Krymov to go the Petrograd to stop the Bolshevik takeover.

When Kerensky heard that Krymov was leading troops northward, he assumed that they were attempting a coup. Together with the Soviet, he armed soldiers and workers alike in Petrograd, supposedly to defend the government against Kornilov's counterrevolution. Some workers, soldiers, and agitators also traveled southward to cut off railroad lines to slow the troops down. As news from Petrograd slowly reached Kornilov's men, it became apparent that there was no Bolshevik threat. The troops dissolved, and there was relatively little violence.

Kerensky summoned Krymov to the capital. The pair conversed briefly — the contents of their interaction are unknown, but shortly after it ended, Krymov shot himself. Kornilov, along with several other military leaders, was arrested shortly thereafter.

Aftermath of the Kornilov affair

Kerensky had hoped that his fight against Kornilov would paint him as a valiant defender of Russia's future democracy. Instead, it became clear that he could not control Russia. Many average workers saw the whole spectacle as a silly spat between two powerful men and weren't particularly inclined to support Kerensky now that it was over.

At the same time, Kornilov's downfall led to a total collapse of discipline within the military. The affair had increased suspicion among Russia's troops, and the rate of desertion substantially increased.

Politically, the Bolsheviks seemed to benefit most from the affair. They had supported Kerensky over Kornilov but had little intention of continuing to do so. On August 31, 1917, they won a majority of seats in the Petrograd Soviet. And with Kornilov out of the picture, and many people losing faith in Kerensky, Russia was facing a large power vacuum. The question was, who would fill it?

Chapter 6:
The Second Uprising

"To delay will be fatal."[1]

That was the message from Vladimir Lenin to his Bolshevik colleagues in October 1917. Lenin was still hiding in Finland, where he had been since the July Days. But he believed that, when it came to revolution, the Bolsheviks could wait no longer. In Petrograd, the empire's political stability was deteriorating fast. Public faith in the Provisional Government — which was never particularly high — continued to drop following the Kornilov affair. Though the Bolsheviks had tentatively supported Kerensky against Kornilov in August, they were now interested in seizing power themselves.

Russia had already experienced one revolution in 1917. Now, it was time for another. As the Julian calendar turned to October, the Bolsheviks were ready to go.

---

1   Ascher, 105.

Fast Fact: Kerensky, nervous and paranoid during the last few months of his tenure as prime minister, took morphine and cocaine to help himself cope with the stress.[2]

Elections and Rebellions

The Bolsheviks thought they could achieve a revolution in part because they had been doing well in recent elections. In Moscow, they went from winning 11 percent of votes in local elections in May 1917 to 51 percent of votes in September.[3] In Petrograd, they finally achieved a majority of the seats in the Soviet after elections on September 25.

The Bolsheviks also felt empowered by the growth of peasant rebellions in rural Russia. Lenin had previously been reluctant to carry out a revolution because he didn't feel the countryside was ready, and he didn't want to start a civil war. However, the revolutionary spirit seemed to be spreading throughout Russia — word trickled back to Petrograd that peasants in the countryside were seizing land from their landlords, often with violence. Many of the soldiers who deserted the army were peasants, when they returned home — often with weapons — they helped further this cause. A union between the angry peasants of the countryside and the angry workers of the city seemed like a natural course of action.

---

2   Figes, 456.
3   Figes, 457.

Bolshevik promises

Most of Russia's average peasants and workers didn't know about Karl Marx or communism — they just knew they didn't like the current government. To garner support, the Bolsheviks made numerous promises to various groups. After a Bolshevik revolution, they said, peasants would be able to seize the land and workers could take over the factories. The new government would immediately make peace with Germany. The Bolsheviks also promised that they would allow ethnic minorities — people who lived in the Russian empire but who were not Russia — to secede from Russia and form their own countries.

Many of these promises would be impossible to achieve; others didn't even align with Lenin or the Bolshevik's actual political ideology. Still, the Bolshevik's promises seemed attractive to many Russian citizens.

Trotsky takes the wheel

Leon Trotsky was a Russian scholar and political activist. Like Lenin, he was interested in Marxism, although the two men had their share of disagreements. When Lenin divided Russia's Marxists into Mensheviks and Bolsheviks at the 1905 Congress, Trotsky preferred not to identify as either.

At the outbreak of the February Revolution, Trotsky had been in New York, where he worked as a journalist. He had returned to Russia in May and was appointed to the Executive Committee of the Petrograd Soviet. He also aligned himself with the Bolsheviks and reconciled with Lenin. The two men agreed to work together in planning Russia's second revolution.

In the background of the Bolsheviks' planning, Russia was still fighting in the First World War. On October 9, Trotsky became the leader of a group called the Military Revolutionary Committee. Technically, the organization's purpose was to protect Petrograd in the event of a German invasion. In reality, its members were planning an uprising.

Though many people were suspicious of the Bolsheviks' plans, Trotsky tried to keep quiet about the possibility of an uprising. When, during a session of the Soviet, he was asked whether the Bolsheviks were preparing to seize power, he answered that the Bolsheviks were preparing the means to seize power, but had not actually decided to do so.

Decision time

The Congress of Soviets was scheduled for October 20, 1917. At this meeting, representatives from Soviets all across Russia would meet and discuss their plans for the future. Lenin didn't want to wait until the Congress to vote on the Bolsheviks' plans for revolution. With several other Bolshevik leaders, he planned a special session of the Soviet's Central Committee on October 10.

The 21 members of the Central Committee met on October 10 at the Smolny Institute in Petrograd. Still fearing for his safety,

Lenin shaved his beard and wore a wig to avoid detection by policeman.

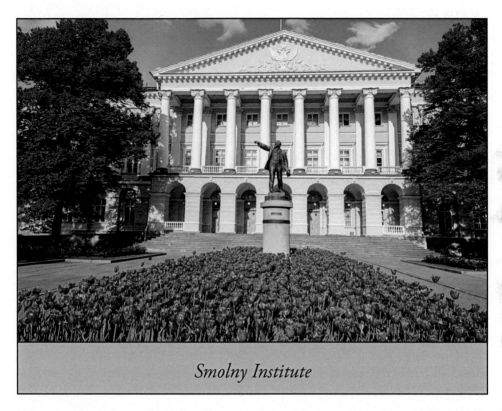

Smolny Institute

The meeting lasted ten hours. In the end, Lenin's proposal, calling for an immediate revolution, passed 19 votes to two votes.[4] The measure was fairly vague. It didn't set a date or say how such a revolution would be carried out. Trotsky recommended that the revolution wait a little longer. He wanted to make sure the Bolsheviks had the support of the Soviet, which he thought would make the uprising more legitimate.

Lenin didn't want to wait. He thought the Soviet's opinion was irrelevant, but the majority of the members of the Central

Committee supported Trotsky, and Lenin ultimately agreed to follow their decision and consult the Soviet.

The decision to launch a revolution was not without controversy. Two members of the Central Committee — Grigory Zinoviev and Lev Kamenev — had opposed Lenin's proposal; after the vote, Kamenev resigned from the committee. On October 18, he published an editorial arguing that an armed Bolshevik uprising would be a mistake. Kamenev's public campaign against the revolution meant that the Bolsheviks' plans were no longer secret.

Lenin was furious. In a series of angry letters, he called for Zinoviev and Kamenev to both be expelled from the party. Aware of the Bolsheviks' plans, the leaders of the Soviet decided to postpone their Congress until October 25. They thought that a few extra days would help calm the situation. Regardless, the Bolsheviks continued to prepare for the revolution.

The Second Revolution

One of the most surprising aspects of the Bolshevik revolution is how little the Provisional Government did to stop it. Kerensky seemed to underestimate the Bolsheviks' power — he thought an uprising would simply be a repeat of the July Days and didn't bother to arrest any Bolshevik leaders.

"I have greater forces than necessary," he told one of his advisors on October 20. "They will be utterly crushed."[5]

---

5   Figes, 480.

He was very wrong.

The Bolshevik takeover

On October 24, the day before the Congress of Soviets, Kerensky shut down the *Rabochii Put*, a Bolshevik newspaper. This relatively minor action was the exact provocation that the Bolsheviks were waiting for. That same day, Trotsky ordered armed Bolsheviks to occupy several government buildings and called for Kerensky to surrender.

Kerensky thought he had the forces to take on a Bolshevik uprising. In reality, few showed up to defend him. Many soldiers decided to stay in their barracks rather than support the Provisional Government. Armed groups of workers and soldiers — known as the Red Guards — took to the streets, taking over police stations, the state bank, and the city's electricity facility. By morning, the Bolsheviks controlled almost all of Petrograd, with the exception of the central area around the Winter Palace, where Kerensky and his ministers were still camped out. Since the Bolsheviks had taken over Petrograd's electricity station, the remaining members of the Provisional Government could not even control their own lights.[6]

The final stage of the Bolshevik takeover occurred on the evening of October 25, 1917. It was not a dramatic affair. Most of the forces who had been defending the Winter Palace had already gone home. The Military Revolutionary Committee, which was responsible for the assault, insisted on waiting for some Baltic

6   Figes, 482.

sailors, who arrived late. Then, they were planning to use field guns from the Peter and Paul Fortress, which turned out to actually be museum pieces which could not be fired.

Kerensky — fearing for his safety — had already snuck out of the Winter Palace in the morning of October 25. When Bolshevik forces finally stormed the building at around 2 a.m. on October 26, they found only a few remaining ministers. The ministers were placed under arrest, and escorted to the Peter and Paul Fortress, where they would be imprisoned. They had to walk because the Bolsheviks didn't have a car.[7]

Fast Fact: Kerensky, disguised as a female nurse, managed to escape by car from the Winter Palace and Petrograd. He later moved to Paris.

The Congress of Soviets

As the Bolsheviks were stumbling through their attack on the Winter Palace, the Congress of Soviets was set to open at a nearby building called the Smolny. Lenin had wanted the Winter Palace to fall before the Congress of Soviets began so he could open the Congress with a dramatic announcement. As the Military Revolutionary Committee continued to postpone the final attack, the Bolsheviks continued to postpone the beginning of the Congress. The delegates were getting restless. Eventually, the Bolsheviks realized they could wait no longer, and the Congress

---

7   Figes, 491.

finally opened around 10:40 p.m., even though the Winter Palace had not yet fallen.[8]

The Bolsheviks did not have a majority in the Soviet, but they thought that they would be able to get their measures through by aligning with the Mensheviks and the Socialist-Revolutionaries. Julian Martov, a Menshevik, proposed a coalition government, whereby representatives from each of the parties would work together to rule. But it only took a few minutes for this vision to fall apart.

Several Mensheviks and Socialist-Revolutionaries stood up and denounced the Bolsheviks' assault on the Provisional Government, saying it would likely cause a civil war. The Bolsheviks — who did not want to be criticized — expressed contempt for the other socialist parties. In a crucial moment, Martov and many of his allies stood up and walked out of the Congress.

While the Mensheviks and Socialist-Revolutionaries intended their walk-out as a form of political protest, leaving effectively took away their power and influence. Trotsky proposed a resolution condemning those who had left as traitors attempting to undermine the revolution.

It was late at night and the Congress was in chaos. The majority of delegates probably had no idea what Trotsky's resolution meant. But Trotsky was a powerful speaker and he managed to pass the resolution with fervent support from the remaining delegates.

8   Figes, 489.

The Bolsheviks had effectively created a single-party state. Decisions about the future of Russia fell to them alone.

Beyond Petrograd

As with the uprisings against the tsar in February, the most notable events of the October Revolution seemed to occur in Petrograd. However, the Bolsheviks realized that their revolution would not be successful if they only acted in the capital city, so they coordinated similar uprisings in other cities. Moscow was particularly important — Lenin knew that the Bolsheviks would not be recognized as legitimate rulers if they did not have control of the city. The Moscow Duma — which remained loyal to the Provisional Government — organized students and soldiers to fight back against the Military Revolutionary Committee. Both sides fired shots in the streets and many civilians were caught up in the crossfire, but after nearly a week of fighting, the tide turned in favor of the Bolsheviks.

Although the Bolsheviks had a dedicated group of supporters, they still encountered plenty of opposition. Even once they were able to take control of local governments, the fight wasn't over. Mikhail Vasiliev-Iuzhin, Bolshevik party chairman in the Russian city of Saratov, noted a major problem the Bolsheviks faced:

"The enemies we released almost immediately went to the Don, to the Urals, to the Caucasus and Ukraine in order to set up regular counterrevolutionary armies against us."[9]

9   Daly and Trofminov, 120.

The Bolsheviks had seized power. But their enemies were still lurking.

The early Bolshevik government

Lenin had spent much of his life writing and arguing in favor of communism in Russia. Now, he seemed to have the power to bring his vision to his country. However, Lenin and most of his Bolshevik allies had no experience governing a nation. They began to provide a hint as to what new Russia would look like, but they quickly encountered problems.

The civil servants problem

Alexandra Kollontai was the first People's Commissar of Social Welfare after the Bolshevik seizure of power. No Russian woman had held such a position before, which posed a problem for Kollontai when she showed up for her first day at work: the doorman refused to let her in.[10]

As it turned out, Kollontai's problem wasn't just her gender. In the first few weeks of Bolshevik power, many former civil servants — people working in lower-level government positions — refused to cooperate with the Bolsheviks, viewing the new regime as illegitimate. These government employees protested in a variety of ways, such as removing office furniture, stealing pens, and simply refusing to work.

One of the biggest obstacles the Bolsheviks faced was taking over the State Bank and Treasury. The new government needed to pay

10   Figes, 500.

people — but they were denied access to the old government's money. The Bolsheviks did not seize control of the State Bank until mid-November in an operation that looked suspiciously like a bank robbery.

Most Bolshevik officials already lacked experience working in government. Without the cooperation of government employees, they looked weak and incompetent. They would need to act decisively to prove they were really able to control Russia.

Economic and social programs

Bolshevik parade during the Russian Revolution; Spring 1917. Aligned against the Provisional Government headed by Kerensky.

On the question of land reform, Lenin agreed to redistribute all land to the peasants. Lenin and his Bolshevik followers did not favor land redistribution — they preferred the nationalization of land, bringing it under government control. However, they realized that the redistribution of farmland was necessary to win over the peasants, who were still Russia's largest social class. To win over industrial workers, Lenin also promised to reorganize the economic system in a way that would give workers control over industry and factories.

The early Bolshevik government also instituted a number of social reforms. All officers in the army were stripped of their rank and it was decided that soldiers would elect their officers instead. Additionally, the Bolsheviks eliminated many of Russia's outdated marriage and divorce laws, which had deprived women of equal rights.

Political power

When it came to political reform, the Bolsheviks were less willing to compromise. On October 27, they announced a temporary ban on newspapers that were critical of their regime. In December, they founded the Cheka, a secret police with the task of eliminating opposition to the new government. The name Cheka came from the abbreviation for "All-Russian Extraordinary Commission to Combat Counter-Revolution and Sabotage."

The terms "counter-revolution" and "counter-revolutionary" were commonly used in Russia in the aftermath of the revolution.

There was a fear that someone — anyone — would try to turn back time, so these words became like accusations. Fear of a counter-revolution was often used to justify many anti-freedom measures.

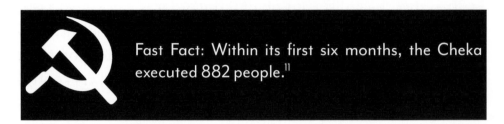

Fast Fact: Within its first six months, the Cheka executed 882 people.[11]

November elections

Elections for Russia's Constituent Assembly were set to take place in November. The Constituent Assembly had never met before — it had been promised after the February Revolution, but elections had been postponed several times.

Lenin had little interest in a Constituent Assembly. He was uninterested in the opinions of average Russians and he figured that some members of the bourgeoisie would likely be elected to the assembly. However, Lenin's new government knew that attempting to prevent the elections would be a bad idea. When the Bolsheviks had seized power a few weeks earlier, they had claimed their revolution was necessary that the Provisional Government would never let the Constituent Assembly meet. For the Bolsheviks to prevent such a meeting now that they were in charge would have been political suicide.

The election was essentially a referendum on the Bolsheviks' revolution. If the Bolsheviks won a majority of seats in the

11   Ascher, 113.

Constituent Assembly, they could genuinely say that they had the support of the people. Many optimistic Bolshevik leaders believed that this would be the case.

The voting began on November 12, 1917, and lasted two weeks — because Russia was so large, different regions had to vote at different times. The results were not great for the Bolsheviks. In total, Lenin's party won about a quarter of the votes, mostly in cities like Petrograd and Moscow. The Socialist Revolutionary Party won the most votes, with 38 percent. The SRs had been divided on the issue of the revolution — some of them had supported the Bolshevik takeover, while others had opposed it — so the meaning of their victories for the Bolsheviks was unclear. The Kadets — who had opposed the revolution — also did fairly well in the elections.

The Bolshevik response to the results was not encouraging for Russia's future as a democracy. Rather than allow the new members of the Constituent Assembly to meet as planned, the Bolshevik government suspended the assembly indefinitely. The Military Revolutionary Committee arrested three of the assembly's electoral commissioners and replaced them with Bolsheviks.

On November 28, a group of protestors staged a demonstration outside Tauride Palace, demanding that the assembly be allowed to meet. In response, the Bolsheviks immediately denounced the protest as a counter-revolutionary conspiracy organized by the Kadets and outlawed the Kadet Party.

The Constituent Assembly did eventually meet — for 13 hours on January 5 and 6, 1918. When deputies returned on January 8, however, they found that the assembly had been dissolved. The Bolsheviks needed a way to maintain power. It appeared that their method would be silencing their political opponents.

Chapter 7: Bolshevik Russia

The Bolsheviks' initial moves had focused on securing their power over Russia. But Russia was also facing major crises, and the new government had to ensure that there would still be a country for them to govern. In particular, the Bolshevik government had to find Russia a way out of the First World War and fix a broken Russian economy. Neither would be an easy task.

No More War

On October 26, 1917 — just after the Bolshevik seizure of power — Lenin read a proclamation to the Congress of Soviets. Called the "Proclamation to the Peoples of All the Belligerent Nations," Lenin's speech asked not only for an end to the war, but for peace without annexations or indemnities — meaning that countries who stopped fighting wouldn't take land from each other or force one another to pay money. In the spirit of the revolution, Lenin's speech was not directed at political leaders, but at average people across Europe. If the citizens of France and Germany and Britain and Austria-Hungary all revolted, Lenin believed, it would force their leaders into peace talks.

Lenin's proclamation was met with massive applause by members of the Congress of Soviets. Soldiers in the audience burst into tears.[1] Across Russia, many people were sick and tired of the war and grateful that the new government wanted to end it.

Unfortunately for Lenin and the Russian soldiers and workers who supported him, ending Russia's involvement in the First World War would take more than a proclamation. Calling for peace was nice, but achieving it would be much harder.

Discussions with Germany

The German and Russian governments agreed to a temporary ceasefire on November 20, 1917. Both countries needed a break — the Bolsheviks needed to fulfill their promise of ending the war, while Germany was still battling France and its allies in Western Europe. However, when the two countries tried to negotiate a permanent end to Russia's involvement in the war, there was little agreement.

On December 27, Trotsky led a Russian delegation to Brest-Litovsk, the city which housed the German military headquarters. The negotiations got off to a rough start when Russian delegates were caught passing out socialist leaflets to German soldiers, encouraging them to prepare for a socialist revolution.[2] Matters only worsened for Trotsky and his delegates when the Germans proposed their peace plan, which called for Russia to give up a significant portion of its western territory to Germany. Shocked

1   Figes, 537.
2   Ascher, 115.

at this request, Trotsky insisted on returning to Petrograd to discuss the matter with other Bolshevik leaders.

The Bolshevik version of peace

Upon Trotsky's return, Lenin urged the Bolsheviks to accept the German peace terms. He thought that the Bolsheviks needed to focus on securing their power over Russia — the war only distracted from this mission. But other Bolshevik leaders were less convinced.

Emboldened by their success in Russia, some Bolsheviks thought that the revolution would soon spread to other parts of Europe. They argued that making peace with the German government was silly — it was better to wait until German communist revolutionaries overthrew their own government. The fliers that Trotsky had handed out to German soldiers fit into this plan. Lenin himself had even argued for it; the peace proclamation he made in October had essentially asked common people to revolt against their own governments.

The Bolshevik vision for peace in Europe wasn't just about ending the slaughter. Rather, the Bolsheviks wanted to achieve peace via revolutions in other countries. To do so, they would need more time. After considerable discussion, the Bolshevik Central Committee — despite Lenin's opposition — agreed to reject the German peace deal and increase support for communist agitation in Germany. Nikolai Ivanovich Bukharin — who had advocated strongly for such a plan — argued that the possibility of a communist revolution would frighten the

German government and force them to reevaluate the peace deal.

In response to the Germans, Trotsky announced a Russian policy known as "neither war nor peace." Russia would not fight a war, but they would not sign a peace agreement either.

The final agreement

The German government was not impressed by Trotsky's "neither war nor peace" policy. Seeing Russia's weakness, German military commanders ordered a new offensive and advanced even further into Russia.

The new attack led Trotsky to change his mind. In another vote, the Central Committee agreed to accept the terms of the peace deal. On March 3, 1918, German and Russian leaders signed the Treaty of Brest-Litovsk. The treaty forced Russia give up a lot: it lost 26 percent of its population, 32 percent of its yearly crop yield, and a whopping 75 percent of its coal mines.

The loss of agricultural and industrial resources proved incredibly damaging for the Russian economy, but Bolshevik leaders weren't too concerned. Many of them were idealists and thought that their success indicated that the tide was turning in favor of communism across Europe. They genuinely believed that Germany would still soon experience its own communist revolution and the treaty would become irrelevant.

While Germany did experience significant political turmoil in the following years, it would not see a revolution. Nor would any other European country. The Bolsheviks guessed wrong.

 Fast Fact: Lenin threatened to resign if the Bolshevik Central Committee did not accept the German peace deal the second time.[3]

You're not Russian anymore

To Lenin and other members of the Bolshevik Central Committee, agreeing to the German peace terms was a necessary step, even if it was difficult. But for the 55 million Russian citizens who lived in the roughly one million square miles of territory that Russia gave up, the treaty meant that they were no longer part of the empire.

The areas that make up Lithuania, Courland (Latvia), Estonia, Finland, Poland, and Ukraine (which had belonged to the Russian Empire) officially became independent, although Germany had significant influence over them. Some residents were happy about this — they had opposed the Bolshevik government, and now they had a chance to be an independent country.

In other places, there was significant opposition to the expansion of German influence. Hundreds of thousands of German and Austrian troops occupied Ukraine, taking its grain and sending

3   Figes, 547.

it back to hungry people in their own countries. Ukrainian peasants weren't happy — they began revolting and launching guerilla attacks on German troops and railroads.

The Ukrainian countryside was in chaos. Luckily for Lenin and the Bolsheviks, it wasn't their problem anymore.

Economic Problems

On February 20, 1918, one Russian solider sent Lenin a letter.

"I would like to ask you as leader of the proletariat: what is going to happen next?" he wrote. "There is no bread, no flour, no potatoes, nothing to eat, and by the way, new mouths keep coming and coming. But, comrade Lenin, I am asking you, what is going to happen next?"[4]

Many Russian citizens were starving. Their country was running out of basic goods like food and the people were counting on the new government to come through and save the day.

 Fast Fact: Communists used the word "comrade" to refer to one another, as it implied that they were equals. It was normal for even peasants to refer to Lenin as a comrade.

---

4   Daly and Trofminov, 171.

The struggle to produce

In March 1918, the Bolsheviks rebranded, deciding to refer to themselves as "communists." It was a more recognizable name — "Bolshevik" was a word that Lenin himself had created while the word "communist" referred to communism, an actual economic concept.

In terms of economics, however, Russia wasn't doing so well. The country simply wasn't producing as much as it needed — it couldn't grow enough wheat and potatoes or make enough manufactured goods (things like cars and farming tools that were created in factories) to support its population. It was a big problem — and one that the Bolsheviks themselves had partially created.

Workers in charge

In November 1917, the new government placed workers in charge of Russia's factories. They were fulfilling one of the key components of Marxist ideology — the proletariat, not the bourgeoisie, would control the means of production.

Unfortunately, placing the workers in charge of Russian factories didn't work out so well in reality. Workers who had spent their lives operating machines or repeating simple manual tasks didn't know how to make decisions about producing goods efficiently. As a result, Russia's already low industrial production plummeted even further.

An abandoned Russian factory.

Running out of food

Russia's terrible industrial production had consequences for the rest of the economy, too, including the production of food. Because Russian manufacturing was doing so poorly, many people in cities could not afford to pay very much for grain. When peasants in the countryside saw that the price of grain was low, they decided to not sell their grain to the cities, as they wouldn't make a profit.

Other factors only worsened the problem. The treaty with Germany certainly hurt. Russia had given up many of its most profitable mines and best farmland. The economic problems that had plagued Russia during the war also hadn't gone away.

Since a lot of Russian peasants had been drafted into the army, and many of them died fighting, some fields simply went to waste.

Making matters worse, Russia's terrible transportation system made it difficult and expensive to get goods from one place to another. The workers and the soldiers — the very people who Lenin and his party claimed to help — were starving. The government had to act.

War Communism

In June 1918, Lenin introduced a radical economic plan called War Communism. The plan attempted to address Russia's low production levels by having the government make all the decisions about what was produced. Private enterprise, where people could buy and sell goods from others, was made illegal.

When it came to grain production, peasants were no longer allowed to grow and sell the amount that they wanted. Instead, according to a part of War Communism called Prodrazvyorstka, they were required to give all their grain — above a certain low amount — to the government. Committees of peasants enforced these rules.

War Communism also created strict rules for workers. Social classes that had not previously worked, like the aristocracy, were required to do so. Strikes — once a powerful tool against the tsar — were forbidden.

The money problem

After the Bolsheviks took over Russia's banks in November 1917, the new government printed a lot of money. Printing money seemed necessary — after all, the government had to pay for things. However, as the government printed more and more currency to pay salaries or buy weapons, the value of the money decreased dramatically.

As money became nearly worthless in Russia, the government started to use goods as a form of currency instead. People began to receive their wages in the form of food or other goods and pay their taxes the same way. By 1921, 94 percent of workers in Russia received goods, not money, as their salary.[5]

Did War Communism work?

The goal of Lenin's War Communism was to increase Russia's production. It failed spectacularly. Peasants in the countryside didn't want to give up their grain to the government, so they produced only the minimum amount. By 1921, Russia's total agricultural production was 54 percent less than it had been in 1913.[6] As a result of food shortages, many Russians began to move from cities back to the countryside. Between 1917 and 1920, Moscow and Petrograd each lost about half of their populations.

---

5   Ascher, 122.
6   Ascher, 123.

Starvation was the reality for many Russians from 1918 onward. Over the next few years, roughly seven million Russian citizens died from malnutrition or disease.

 Fast Fact: An epidemic of Spanish Flu broke out in Russia and across the world in 1918. While estimates about the total number people the flu killed vary, some experts believe it may have been responsible for the deaths of roughly 50 million people between 1918 and 1920.[7]

War Communism, war politics

While Lenin had announced War Communism as an economic program, the policy also had substantial political effects. In particular, it signaled even more government control over the citizens of Russia. The Bolsheviks had already limited many political freedoms — banning newspapers and using secret police to keep the opposition quiet. Now, the communist government was also limiting workers' control over their own livelihoods.

The name itself, "War Communism," was also quite telling. Although Russia had just pulled out of a world war, the nation was quickly finding itself in another conflict. This time, it would be a civil war.

---

7   Taubenberger and Morens, 15.

Chapter 8: Civil War

At the beginning of the First World War, the Austro-Hungarian Empire had sent a group of Czech soldiers to fight Russia on the Eastern front. Though the Czechs technically fell under the rule of Austria-Hungary, many Czech soldiers felt no loyalty to the empire. In 1917, a brigade of these soldiers, which included roughly 45,000 men, decided to rebel and fight against the Central Powers. They hoped that if they helped the Allies succeed and win the war, they might be able to secure Czech independence afterwards.

There was just one problem with the plan. In 1918, these politically-minded soldiers were still stuck in Russia. The Eastern front of the war no longer existed because Russia had pulled out of the war. If the Czech soldiers wanted to fight, they needed to get to France, where the conflict was still raging.

The shortest route to France would require the soldiers to pass through Austria-Hungary, something that the Austro-Hungarian Empire (which was fighting France) would not allow. The Russian government, who didn't particularly want the Czech soldiers in Russia, agreed to allow them to travel east through Russia to the port of Vladivostok on the Pacific Ocean, where they could sail to France. However, not thrilled about the prospect of Czech soldiers marching through the country, the Russian government attached one condition to this offer: they asked that the soldiers turn over most of their weapons.

The Czech soldiers didn't want to give up their weapons. In a fateful move, Trotsky ordered Russian troops to disarm the Czech troops by any means necessary. When the Russian army attempted to do so, the Czechs fought back. In May 1918, a series of clashes broke out in the Ural Mountains, and by the first week of June, the Czech soldiers had taken over several Russian towns.

The Czechs, as it turned out, were one of the many parties who would become involved in the Russian Civil War. It's difficult to say exactly when the war began. Some historians set the war's start date to October 26, 1917, the day after the Bolsheviks took power. While violent conflicts did erupt between the Bolsheviks and their enemies after October 26, an organized war with armies fighting on two distinct sides truly began during the summer of 1918.[1]

Given the involvement of the Czech soldiers and several other foreign armies who would later fight in Russia, the conflict wasn't really a civil war either. But the start date and the official name of the Russian Civil War were ultimately minor details compared to its devastating effects. By the time the conflict petered out in 1922, millions of Russian citizens would die of war, disease, and starvation.

In 1918, another war seemed like the last thing Russia needed. Unfortunately, it was exactly what the country got.

---

1   Fitzpatrick, 74.

Fast Fact: Russia switched from the Julian to the Gregorian Calendar in early 1918. To account for this change, the government declared that the calendar skipped from January 31 to February 14. The dates in between never happened in Russia in 1918.[2]

Who is Fighting Who?

The Russian Civil War involved numerous groups with a variety of goals. Sometimes they formed alliances together; sometimes they went back on their promises and attacked one another. Some soldiers fought for ideas they strongly believed in; others fought because they had been ordered to do so. At times, armies conducted organized campaigns and met on battlefields; at times, they engaged in guerilla warfare and it became unclear who was fighting on what side.

Although much of the Russian Civil War was marked by confusion and chaos, the parties involved in the conflict are typically broken down into a few main groups.

Reds vs. Whites

The two main sides in the Russian Civil War were known by colors, the Reds and the Whites. The color red seemed like an obvious choice for the communists — since the French Revolution in 1789, red was supposed to represent the blood of workers who had died in the struggle against capitalism.

---

2   Figes, xxi.

The early communist army (also known as the Red Army) was mostly made up of members of the Red Guard, who had helped the Bolsheviks seize power from the Provisional Government in October 1917. They were joined by army units who had expressed loyalty to the communist government. When these soldiers were still not enough, the government began to draft peasants and workers into the Red Army.

Most of the common workers and soldiers were not officers and had little experience with military strategy. As a result, the communist government also relied on many of the tsar's former officers. Everyone ultimately fell under the command of Trotsky, who became Russia's Commissar of War in early 1918.

On their path to power, the Bolsheviks made plenty of enemies. The groups that chose to fight back against the communist government were loosely known as the Whites — the color white had referred to the monarchy during the French Revolution. The groups that made up the Whites came from very different places and had very different ideas. However, they had one common goal: they wanted to see the communists defeated.

Who were the Whites?

The Whites consisted mainly of five different political groups. The tsarists wanted to see the return of a monarch with absolute power; the Octobrists wanted the monarchy back, but with limited power; the Kadets wanted a democracy; Socialist Revolutionaries who had opposed the Bolshevik takeover wanted a democracy and the redistribution of land to the peasants;

and various ethnic minorities wanted their independence from Russia.

The White Army began to take shape in December 1917, when two men — General Kornilov (who had attempted a coup against Kerensky) and Anton Denikin — escaped from prison and started to gather followers in southern Russia. Kornilov was killed in April 1918, so Denikin became the main commander of White troops in the south.

In Siberia, the White Army fell under the command of Alexander Kolchak, who had been a commander in the imperial Russian navy under Nicholas II. Both Denikin and Kolchak faced many difficulties. Their locations — far away from Russia's major cities — made it hard for them to transport troops, receive supplies, and communicate with one another.

In addition to these logistical problems, Denikin and Kolchak also had to deal with trying to govern a divided group of people. Denikin, who was deeply nationalist, wanted to see a united Russia, and therefore didn't work well with ethnic minority groups who were seeking independence. His supporters also weakened his case for unity by reclaiming peasant land and attacking Jewish towns.[3]

The other sides

Not everyone in the Russian Civil War fell under the banner of Reds and Whites. Some people tried to stay out of the conflict

3   Ascher, 130.

entirely. Others decided to fight against both the communist government and the White Army.

One notable third-party group was the Free Territorial Society, a subset of Ukrainian nationalists. Their leader was a man named Nestor Makhno. He opposed any government authority, leading Denikin to call them anarchists. Makhno and his followers were known for their brutal tactics and their use of guerilla warfare. They were not opposed to attacking innocent civilians. At times, they aligned themselves with the Red Army against the Whites, although Trotsky later turned on them.

Some peasants also banded together to look out for their own interests. These groups, known as green armies, largely worked to protect peasant land. Although they supported neither the Reds nor the Whites, they were largely located in rural Russia, and therefore they mostly ended fighting against the White Army while leaving the Reds alone.

The Russian Civil War, as it turned out, wasn't just limited to Russians. Several other countries — each with their own goals and military strategies — would soon enter the conflict as well.

Foreign Intervention

The early Czech military victories convinced several other countries that involving themselves in Russia's conflict was a good idea. The new Russian government and its army looked very weak. If a bunch of unorganized traveling Czech soldiers could easily take over Russian towns, then the world's major powers with their professional armies would have no trouble achieving their goals.

The fight against communism

So what did other countries want when they decided to join Russia's civil war?

Countries like Britain and France were worried about communism, particularly about the potential for a communist takeover in Germany. While war was raging in Russia, Germany was facing dire problems of its own. The nation had lost the First World War, and the Treaty of Versailles — which had formally concluded the war in 1919 — had been incredibly harsh. Germany seemed to be falling apart.

Germany's fragility was one of the reasons that Lenin thought communism might spread to the country. But where Lenin saw an opportunity, many Western European countries saw the potential for disaster. Britain, France, and their allies believed that communism posed a huge threat to the kind of world they were trying to create.

The way to prevent the spread of communism, they thought, was to attack the problem at its root. If they overthrew the communist government in Russia, then surely they would stamp out communism once and for all.

The countries that intervened against Russia's communist government didn't see themselves as meddling foreigners, but as supporters of the White Army. In a letter to a French official in 1919, a young British politician named Winston Churchill wrote: "We ought to do our utmost to weave together and take the lead of all the anti-Bolshevik forces that exist, and to give them the material and moral aid which they require."[4]

Fast Fact: The Treaty of Versailles was incredibly harsh on Germany, forcing the nation to disarm its military, give up territory, and pay reparations to the countries it had just lost to. When German officials argued that these terms were unfair, Britain and France pointed to the Treaty of Brest-Litovsk and the harsh conditions that Germany had forced on Russia a year earlier.

Other motives

While Churchill talked of defeating the Bolsheviks, there were certainly other motives for foreign intervention in the Russian Civil War. For many years, historians have speculated about other reasons why European countries chose to involve themselves in the war. Some have argued that Britain, for example, was hoping for eventual economic profits in Siberia.[5] Other historians have argued that the European intervention in Russia was mostly due to confusion and small, uncoordinated military plans.[6]

European countries weren't the only ones to intervene in the Russian Civil War. Japan — which had shocked the world when it had defeated Russia in 1905 — was continuing to grow its

4   Daly and Trofminov, 257.
5   Arno, 484.
6   Carley, 413.

empire. Japanese leaders thought that they could take advantage of Russia's chaos to grab some more territory for their empire. Meanwhile, the United States was concerned about Japanese expansion. The American military sent some 13,000 soldiers to Siberia, supposedly to keep Japan in check.[7]

Despite these differing motives, all countries would soon find that the war in Russia was quite costly. As it turned out, their presence wouldn't last.

The costs of war

The Czech soldiers who had been the first foreigners involved in the Russian Civil War quickly grew tired of fighting. They had wanted to go home and fight Germany, not stay in Russia and fight the communist government there. Although the Czechs fought along the White Army for a few months, their units quickly fell apart. Many soldiers deserted, and some — who were sympathetic to the communists — even joined the Red Army.[8] What was left of the Czech army was officially evacuated from Vladivostok in 1920.

The Czechs were hardly the only ones to discover the difficulties of fighting a war in Russia. Countries like Britain and France quickly found that their intervention was unpopular with their own citizens. The First World War had killed millions, proving devastating to a generation of young European men — after that war was over, people didn't want to send their troops to Russia.

7   Ascher, 127.
8   Figes, 581.

The troops that were in Russia made little progress. The armies from different countries found it difficult to coordinate, both with each other and with the White Army. As a result of these struggles, most foreign armies withdrew from Russia by 1921.

The Course of War

The biggest threat to Russia's communist government, as it turned out, was from the White Army, rather than foreign countries. Although the Whites controlled substantial territory in central Russia at their peak, they also faced many disadvantages. As the war continued, the Bolsheviks gained the upper hand — but not without a lot of violence.

Violence and terror

On August 30, 1918, a woman named Fanya Kaplan — who was a member of the Socialist-Revolutionary Party — fired three shots at Lenin, hitting him in the arm and the neck. She was quickly caught and executed a few weeks later. Lenin would recover from the shooting and returned to work in October.

 Fast Fact: When arrested, Kaplan told the Cheka that she had acted alone in her assassination attempt. She was likely tortured, then shot, and her remains were destroyed without a trace.[9]

The attempted assassination of Lenin, along with the actual assassination of a Cheka leader in Petrograd on the very same

9   Figes, 629.

day, triggered a systemic crackdown on opposition that became known as the Red Terror.

According to Lenin, the Red Terror was necessary to wipe out counterrevolutionary forces. But the use of terror at times seemed random and indiscriminate. People might be arrested because they had a friend or a family member who was a suspect, or because someone — anyone — accused them of being counterrevolutionary. At times, the Cheka would round up people for being near the scene of a crime. It was better, Lenin believed, to arrest 100 innocent people than to let one suspected enemy go.

Those who were arrested faced dire consequences. Cheka jails were overcrowded, and prisoners received little food or water.

The Cheka regularly used torture to force people to confess to crimes they might not have committed.

Historians typically say that the Red Terror lasted from 1918 until 1922 — the span of the Russian Civil War. The number of people who were killed by the Cheka during this period is disputed — estimates range anywhere from 12,000 to 140,000.[10]

Of course, the Reds were not the only ones to terrorize civilians. The White Army likewise used torture tactics on its suspected enemies. The White Terror was especially awful for Jews, who Whites regarded as sympathetic to communism. Soldiers in the White Army were often given free rein to pillage (attack and rob) Jewish communities, and whole Jewish towns were destroyed. The number of Jews killed by the White Army during the Russian Civil War is unclear, with estimates ranging from 50,000 to 150,000.[11]

Death of the tsar

Tsar Nicholas II had stayed out of Russian politics following his resignation in March 1917. Initially, the former royal family resided in a palace on the outskirts of Petrograd. They were officially under house arrest — and therefore were not permitted to leave the palace — but they lived in relative comfort.

In August 1917, the family left the capital for the Siberian town of Tobolsk. There was concern that remaining in Petrograd

10   Ascher, 114.
11   Figes, 678.

would be dangerous given Russia's political unrest. In Tobolsk, Nicholas and the rest of his family occupied the old governor's mansion. Isolated from the conflict in the capital, it seemed they would be safe.

The family's situation changed after the Bolshevik takeover. While the Provisional Government under Kerensky had largely treated the former royals with kindness and respect, the Bolsheviks were much less sympathetic. In early 1918, Nicholas and the rest noticed that their guards were more hostile, and their food quality deteriorated. In May, they were transported to the city of Ekaterinburg (also spelled as Yekaterinburg), where the Bolshevik government put them up in a building ominously known as the House of Special Designation (the name is also sometimes translated as the House of Special Purpose).

As the civil war picked up during the summer of 1918, there were rumors that the White Army might try to rescue the tsar. There were people in Russia who wanted to see the monarchy restored, although there is little evidence that any of them had a serious plan to free Nicholas that summer.

Regardless, the communist government decided that the old tsar had to go. Around 1:30 in the morning on July 17, 1918, the local Cheka boss, Yakov Yurovsky, ordered the royal physician to wake Nicholas and his family. They were led to the basement along with their servants, seemingly unaware of what was about to happen — they apparently were told that there was violence in town and they would be safer in the basement. Nicholas carried his hemophilic son, Alexei, who was quite ill after a recent bout of bleeding.

The family was not safe in the basement. Around 2:00 a.m., Yurovsky returned with an eleven-person firing squad and read aloud the execution order, which named not only the tsar, but his wife, his children, and their servants.

Nicholas was confused. His last words were reportedly "What? What?" as he asked Yurovsky to repeat the order.[12] Then the firing began, instantly killing the tsar and his wife. When the smoke cleared after a few minutes, Alexei and his sister Anastasia were still alive. Yurovsky shot Alexei in the head and another guard finished off Anastasia with a bayonet.

News of the tsar's execution was kept relatively quiet. The official government announcement on July 19 mentioned only the death of Nicholas, and claimed that his wife and children were sent to a safe place.[13] The communists, it seemed, didn't want to admit that they had killed the tsar's innocent servants and children.

Rumors swirled about the fate of the tsar and his family until 1926, when Nicholas Sokolov — a Russian who had investigated the royal family's murders before leaving the country — published a book with his findings, which was the first public confirmation of their deaths. Their graves would not be discovered until after the fall of the Soviet regime.

---

12   Figes, 640.
13   Figes, 641.

White losses

Initially, the White Army under Denikin's command scored some impressive victories. By October 1919, they seemed to be threatening to capture Moscow. However, they encountered a series of problems, which ultimately sunk their efforts.

First, the White Army began to run short on supplies and reinforcements. Since the Whites were based in Central Russia, where industry was scarce, they struggled to get enough weapons. Transporting soldiers to the front posed another problem, as the Whites were spread out over large areas. At the end of 1919, the White Army suffered two devastating defeats, near Petrograd and Voronezh, turning the tide in favor of the Reds.

Both Denikin and Admiral Kolchak resigned in early 1920, leaving the White Army in the command of Pyotr Wrangel. Wrangel briefly had success in September of that year, while the Red Army was tied up dealing with Polish nationalists under the command of J. K. Pilsudski. However, the Poles and the Russians signed a ceasefire in October 1920, which allowed the Red Army to turn its full attention to Wrangel's forces in Crimea.

Wrangel's forces retreated rapidly in the face of the Red Army's offensive. They held off just long enough to allow 150,000 refugees to board ships to Constantinople, a city that was at the time under control of British, French, and Italian troops. Wrangel boarded one of the last of these ships on November 14, 1920. His fight against the Red Army was over.

The tragedy of Aleskei Brusilov

Aleksei Brusilov had been a top Russian military commander in the First World War, under both the tsar and the Provisional Government. During the Russian Civil War, he had remained neutral. He firmly opposed the Bolsheviks, but didn't support the attempts to topple them militarily.

When Wrangel and many of his supporters were evacuating to Constantinople, a senior communist military official approached Brusilov with a proposal. A number of Wrangel's officers, he said, were planning not to evacuate. The communists were hoping that they could get these officers to defect to the Red Army, and they wanted Brusilov's help.

The communists asked Brusilov to encourage the officers to defect. He agreed: the officers would likely be killed if they tried to fight the communists. If he convinced them to defect, he would probably save their lives, and their presence in the Red Army might make it a little less radical.

With Brusilov's approval, the communist government dropped thousands of leaflets — signed by Brusilov — encouraging Wrangel's officers to defect. A few days later, however, the government told Brusilov that the plan had failed and the officers had refused.

Brusilov later found out that he had been deceived. Hundreds of officers had read the leaflets and stayed behind, planning to join to the Red Army. Rather than having the opportunity to defect, they were shot on site.

The story of Brusilov and Wrangel's officers is a small footnote in the history of Russia's Civil War. Nonetheless, it exemplified two importance tendencies of the new communist government. First, the communists weren't forgiving to their former enemies. Second, they didn't mind using deceptive tactics to achieve their goals.

Brusilov struggled to forgive himself for the deaths of Wrangel's officers. "God and Russia may judge me," he wrote in 1925. He died shortly thereafter.[14]

Is the war over?

The Reds managed to defeat most of the anti-communist forces by the spring of 1921. The communist government controlled a country similar to the old Russian Empire, although Finland, Lithuania, Latvia, Estonia, and Poland became independent countries, with Poland controlling part of Ukraine. The government also continued to face resistance from militants in Central Asia for another decade.

Just as the Russian Civil War didn't have a clear start date, it didn't have a clear end date either. But even if the dates weren't clear, the outcome was. The communists were now accepted as the legitimate rulers of Russia.

---

14   Figes, 720.

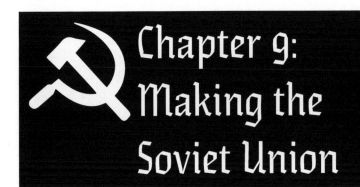

Chapter 9:
Making the
Soviet Union

On New Year's Eve in 1922, the Russian newspaper *Izvestia* had big news: the Congress of Soviets had declared the formation of the Union of Soviet Socialist Republics (also known as the USSR or the Soviet Union).[1] The USSR officially brought together four separate countries — Russia, Belorussia, Ukraine, and Transcaucasia — under one central communist government.[2]

The Communist Party now ruled an area similar to the old Russian Empire. They would stay in power for nearly 70 years.

The New Economic Policy

In 1921, a year before the declaration of the formation of the USSR, Lenin and his communist government were facing several crises. War Communism — Lenin's plan to increase Russia's industrial and agricultural output — had the exact opposite effect, and the country was now facing major shortages. Workers in Petrograd had launched strikes in protest. The Mensheviks,

---

1   Swoboda, 761.
2   Daly and Trofminov, 339.

who were hoping to pressure the government into creating a new constitution, encouraged workers to join the protest and renewed their calls for democracy.

Vladimir Lenin at his desk between 1920 and 1922.

The Kronstadt Rebellion

Seventeen miles west of Petrograd, sailors on a military port called Kronstadt heard news of the unrest. Many of the Kronstadt sailors came from peasant backgrounds, and they had generally been supportive of communism. Lenin had even praised the sailors for their help in the revolutions of 1917.

But now it was 1921, not 1917, and the sailors' support for Lenin's government was dwindling quickly. They had heard about the suffering in the countryside and knew that the communists had failed to fulfill their promises of a better life for Russia's peasants.

When the Kronstadt sailors heard of the protests in Petrograd, they too revolted. In a proclamation, they called for the government to give peasants more freedom on how they used their land, as well as for freedom of speech and new soviet elections.

The sailor's demands were an embarrassment to the communist government. Kronstadt had once been considered a Bolshevik stronghold. Because many of the sailors considered themselves socialists, their betrayal risked a serious split among Russia's communists.[3]

Effects of Kronstadt

The government first demanded that the rebel sailors surrender. When they refused, Trotsky branded them as counterrevolutionaries. His use of this term was significant. By claiming that the sailors were against the revolution, he justified using violence against them in order to protect Russia.

Trotsky then organized an army to storm the Kronstadt military base. The sailors put up a fight, but were ultimately defeated. Thousands of soldiers on each side were killed, and hundreds

3   Ascher, 136.

— perhaps even thousands — of alleged rebels were executed without trial afterwards.

While the sailors failed to achieve their goals, they were successful in one major way: they woke Lenin up to the fact that his economic plans were not working. Soon after the Kronstadt Rebellion, Lenin introduced his New Economic Policy (NEP).

Return to capitalism

The NEP meant big changes for Russia. No longer would the central government control economic decisions. The requirements for peasants to turn over their food to the government were abolished. Instead, peasants were allowed to produce what they wanted and were charged a simple 10 percent tax.[4] Under War Communism, farmers couldn't hire labor or lease machinery. With the NEP, they were allowed to do both of these.

Because of problems with inflation, Russia had virtually stopped using currency during the civil war — people had been paying their taxes and receiving their wages in goods instead. The NEP reintroduced currency. Additionally, trade became legal, meaning that people were allowed to buy or sell to others — previously, all economic transactions had to go through the government.

---

4   Ascher, 138.

Consequences of the NEP

The NEP was a big improvement over War Communism. No longer required to give their crops to the government, peasants began to grow more. The increase in agricultural output helped alleviate food shortages. Russian industry, which was still mostly under government control, was slower to grow. But by 1928, output in most parts of the economy returned to pre-war levels.[5]

Lenin's political maneuvering

Lenin had known that the NEP might be unpopular with many of his fellow communists. The reality was that the NEP was not very communist. Communism implies government control over the means of production in an economy. Although the Russian government still had control over the largest industries and the biggest banks, the NEP meant that they no longer controlled everything that was produced.

To ensure that the Communist Party would approve of the NEP, Lenin changed the rules. In a resolution on the last day of the party's congress, he called for all groups with a platform different than the one of the main party to be expelled. The resolution also gave the Central Committee the authority to expel the people. Lenin said that these changes were necessary because the party was threatened by outsiders.

Lenin's political maneuvering about the passage of the NEP demonstrated his firm grip on political power. Although he was

5   Ascher, 139.

willing to relax some of his controls over the Russian economy, he wouldn't let go of his control over the government.

Life After Lenin

Lenin, as it turned out, wasn't invincible. In May 1922, he suffered his first stroke, which paralyzed the right side of his body and temporarily rendered him unable to speak. While he slowly began to recover, Lenin began to think about who might be his successor as the leader of Russia's communist party.

Meet Josef Stalin

The man who became known as Josef Stalin was born under the name Ioseb Besarionis dze Jughashvili in the Georgian town of Gori in 1879. Georgia had been conquered by the Russian Empire in the early 19th century.

Little is known about Stalin's early life. His father was a shoemaker who died when he was young; his mother sent him to the seminary to study religion. Stalin didn't fit in well at seminary. He was an atheist, and he spent much of his time reading about Marxism. Records show he was caught reading banned books 13 times, and he was ultimately expelled from seminary for missing his exams.[6]

After his expulsion, Stalin read some of Lenin's works and decided to become a revolutionary. He began to organize strikes and coordinate with other Russian socialists, and he was arrested

---

6   Montefiore, 61.

many times. When war broke out in 1914, he was serving time in exile in Siberia. He returned to Petrograd in 1917 after the fall of Tsar Nicholas II and was later elected to the Bolshevik Central Committee.

Fast Fact: Like Lenin, Stalin picked his last name himself. The name Stalin comes from the Russian word for steel.

Stalin vs. Trotsky

Stalin had a deep personal rivalry with fellow prominent communist Leon Trotsky. Both Stalin and Trotsky were members of the Politburo, a group of top communist officials who were largely in charge of running the Soviet Union. During the summer of 1922, Stalin — along with Grigory Zinoviev and Lev Kamenev, also Politburo members — teamed up against Trotsky.

When in 1923 Trotsky called for a greater discussion of national issues among the entire Communist Party, not just the Politburo, Stalin and his allies accused him of being too personally ambitious. A year later, they attacked his ideas, arguing that his vision for a world revolution and global socialism underestimated the strength of the Russian peasantry.

While Stalin came up with many reasons to criticize Trotsky, he was quiet about one of his real motives. Lenin was seriously considering Trotsky as his successor. Stalin wanted that position for himself.

Fast Fact: Stalin spoke Russian with a Georgian accent, which Trotsky privately mocked.[7]

The struggle for power

Lenin returned from his stroke in September 1922, but he was weaker than before. He often left Politburo meetings early, only to discover the next morning that Stalin, Zinoviev, and Kamenev had passed resolutions without him.

Stalin, meanwhile, had taken the position of General Secretary of the Communist Party, which gave him control over many lower party officials. Lenin was worried about Stalin's growing power. In a note to himself on December 24, 1922, he remarked: "Comrade Stalin, having become Secretary-General, has unlimited authority concentrated in his hands, and I am not sure whether he will always be capable of using that authority with sufficient caution."[8]

Lenin hoped that he would be replaced by a group of politicians, rather than any one man. Stalin, however, was a step ahead of him. He convinced the Central Committee and Lenin's doctors that Lenin should be kept in isolation, supposedly to help him

7   Reiber, 1653.
8   Daly and Trofminov, 340.

recover from his health. In reality, keeping Lenin out of the way made it easier for Stalin to control matters in the Politburo.

Lenin's health continued to deteriorate. He died on January 21, 1924. His body was put on display in Moscow's Red Square for several months, so Russians from all over could visit and pay their respects. Soviet leaders then had the idea to preserve his body for the future. Since 1924, generations of Russian scientists have kept the body intact by soaking it in embalming fluids.[9] Lenin's body remains on public display in Moscow today.

 Fast Fact: The city of Petrograd, which was known as St. Petersburg until 1914, underwent another name change 10 years later. After Lenin's death, it was renamed Leningrad in his honor.

Post-Lenin drama

At the time of Lenin's death, it was unclear who would become the new leader of the Soviet Union. Stalin first took action to eliminate Trotsky as a political threat. In 1925, the Politburo forced Trotsky to resign from his position as the Commissariat of War. Realizing he lacked support, Trotsky temporarily left Soviet politics.

Stalin abandoned Zinoviev and Kamenev and found himself new allies. He also persuaded the Communist Party to increase the number of members in the Politburo and ensured that the new appointees were loyal to him.

9   Hsu.

In 1926, Zinoviev, Kamenev, and Trotsky attempted to form an alliance against Stalin, but they were all too politically weak to take him down. Later that year, Stalin managed to oust them from the Politburo. In 1927, he first kicked them out of the Central Committee, and then ultimately the Communist Party.

Stalin later forgave Zinoviev and Kamenev, re-admitting them to the party, although they never regained their former positions. Trotsky, however, was exiled first to Alma-Ata — a city near the Chinese border — and was then kicked out of the country entirely.

Josef Stalin was now the leader of the Soviet Union.

Fast Fact: Trotsky traveled around after leaving the Soviet Union, but Stalin never forgave him. In 1940, Trotsky was living in Mexico when one of Stalin's agents assassinated him with an icepick.

The Early Stalin Days

As Stalin assumed political power in the Soviet Union, it was clear that he was intent on shaping the country himself. Stalin would quickly replace Lenin's NEP with an economic plan of his own. At the same time, when it came to cracking down on political opposition and using violence against his enemies, Stalin turned out to be even more ruthless than his predecessor.

Lenin and Stalin[10]

The five-year plans

In 1927, Stalin — and many of his fellow Soviet leaders — were growing concerned about their nation's standing in the world. Although the NEP had helped boost the economy, Stalin believed that the Soviet Union desperately needed further industrial growth.

Relations between the Soviet Union and its former allies had been tense since the 1917 revolution, and they grew worse during the 1920s. Stalin believed that the capitalist countries of Western Europe might still try to fight the Soviet Union to take

10   Photo Credit: elen_studio / Shutterstock.com

down communism. He needed some rapid industrialization to prepare for this possible conflict.

The first five-year plan

Stalin's first five-year plan, which was enacted in 1928, set specific goals. As a whole, the Soviet Union was supposed to triple its iron output, quadruple its electric power, and double its coal production.

To enforce these production levels, the government took control of the Soviet Union's industries. Every worker was to be an employee of the government — the private enterprise that had existed under Lenin's NEP was gone.

By bringing much of the Soviet Union's economy under government control, Stalin also made it more communist. Some historians argue that in creating an economic system that resembled the Bolshevik plans from 1917, Stalin truly fulfilled the promises of the revolution. Stalin's motives are unclear. While he was a committed communist, he seemed more interested in ensuring his own power than completing the Bolshevik Revolution.

The kulaks and collectivization

The rapid industrialization that Stalin wanted was dependent on a reliable food supply. The Soviet Union's food supply was determined by the peasants in the countryside, who were responsible for producing grain. Under the NEP, peasants could decide how much of their grain to sell and the price they wanted to sell at.

The first five-year plan also called for the collectivization of agriculture, which meant forcing peasants to give up their individual farms and join large group farms. At first, government officials tried to encourage peasants in the countryside to join collective farms voluntarily, but peasants were reluctant and the process was very slow.

Annoyed by the slow pace of collectivization in the countryside, Stalin blamed a group of peasants known as the kulaks. Kulaks were the rich peasants. They weren't a substantial force in Soviet politics; they made up about four percent of the population.[11]

Stalin believed that the kulaks were intentionally hoarding grain, which made them enemies of the Soviet regime. In 1929, when efforts to collectivize farms picked up, Stalin decided that the kulaks would be left out of collectivization — instead, they would be targeted with violence. Beginning in 1930, communist officials went into peasant towns, looking for kulaks. With the help of poor peasants, they would intimidate these rich peasant families, drive them from their homes, and then take their property.

The kulaks weren't the only victims of collectivization. Many peasants, who had enjoyed the freedom of the NEP, killed their own livestock and burned their crops rather than hand them over to the government for collective farms.

---

11   Ascher, 152.

Four years later

Stalin's first five-year plan was supposed to last from 1928 until 1933. However, in 1932, Stalin declared the plan complete — things had gone so well that the country had met its goals in four years rather than five.

How had the Soviet Union made such great progress? In reality, it hadn't. Stalin's numbers were horribly exaggerated. The government didn't have a good way to measure how much coal or iron it was producing; it relied on reporting from workers themselves. Most workers couldn't meet the high goals that the five-year plan had set. But rather than admit that they'd failed, they simply lied about how much they had produced, and the government had no way to check.

The five-year plan wasn't always effective. In some places, factories were built, but there were no machines to fill them. In other places, there were factories and machines, but there weren't any workers who knew how to use the machines.

Despite these problems, the five-year plan did have some impressive achievements. For the first time, the Soviet Union was producing its own automobiles and airplanes. The country was on its way to becoming a major industrial power.

Stalin's political terror

As the episode with the kulaks indicated, Stalin did not mind using violence to intimidate his political opponents. While other leaders such as Russia's tsars, Lenin, and European dictators like Benito Mussolini or Adolf Hitler also used state terror, Stalin was unique in that he did not reserve his use of violence for his political opponents. In fact, Stalin frequently targeted people who shared his ideas.

Historians don't how many people suffered from state terrorism under Stalin's regime, but the number is likely in the millions.[12]

The purges

Much of Stalin's political violence targeted other prominent communists. Stalin's biggest priority seemed to be ensuring that he alone had control of the Soviet Union, and he trusted no one. If he let any of his allies get too powerful, he worried they might overthrow him.

In 1934, Sergei Kirov — who was considered by many to be Stalin's heir — was shot. Many historians speculate that Stalin ordered Kirov killed because he saw Kirov as a rival. A year later, Stalin went after several other leading communists, including his former allies Zinoviev and Kamenev, who were executed.

Stalin's mass-targeting of fellow communists became known as purges. In 1937, for example, he had 90 percent of military generals and 80 percent of colonels arrested and killed.[13]

Stalin would remain the leader of the Soviet Union until his death in 1953.

---

12   Ascher, 165.
13   Ascher, 170.

Chapter 10: The Story Since

The Russian Revolution took place in 1917. The civil war occupied the next few years. The Bolshevik Revolution — their transformation of Russian's political and economic systems — lasted somewhat longer.

The impacts of the Russian Revolution don't stop there. The Soviet Union continued to face questions of government control and leadership that echoed the problems faced by the Bolsheviks in 1917. In the rest of the world, fear of communism and of a Russian-style revolution shaped both local conflicts and global power struggles.

Scary Communism

With the Soviet Union as the world's first communist country, leaders across the world worried that communism would spread to their nations, too. After all, Trotsky had called for a world revolution, and leaders like Lenin had believed that communist revolutions were inevitable in other industrialized countries.

With the threat of communism lurking, some countries seemed to be willing to do anything to prevent it.

Reacting to the Russian Revolution

To foreign leaders who opposed communism, the Russian Revolution seemed to pose two threats. First, there was the possibility that the Soviet Union would actively try to spread communism. The United States, for example, broke off diplomatic relations with Russia in December 1917, and did not re-establish them until 1933.

The second communist threat came from within. If Russia's communists could rise up and take power, it was possible that communists in another country could, too. The United States — and several Western European countries — began to crack down on potential communist threats in their own countries.

Fascism isn't communist!

If countries were fighting against communism, they also needed to be fighting for something. In the United States — which had practiced democracy for nearly 150 years — democracy seemed like an obvious alternative to communism. But in other places, that wasn't so obvious.

Fascism, which preached nationalism and loyalty to the government above all else, emerged as an alternative to communism in countries like Italy, Germany, and Spain. Leaders like Benito Mussolini, who came to power in Italy in 1922, and

Adolf Hitler, who took over in Germany in 1933, portrayed themselves as strong leaders who would save their nations from communism, among other problems.

The conflict between communism and fascism broke out into an actual civil war in Spain in 1936. One side, which was backed by the Soviet Union, included both communists and people who favored democracy. The other side, which was backed by Germany, was largely made up of fascists. The fascists — led by Francisco Franco — won the Spanish Civil War after three years of fighting. Franco would rule Spain until 1975.

To be clear, fear of communism was one of many factors that drove popular support for fascism in Europe. Nonetheless, it's worthwhile to understand that fascist leaders like Mussolini and Hitler made opposition to communism a major part of their ideologies.[1]

The Second World War

The growth of extreme political movements in Europe ending up launching the conflict into its second devastating war of the century. In the late 1930s, Germany — led by Hitler and the Nazi party — began aggressively expanding its territory and targeting racial and ethnic minorities.

In 1939, the Soviet Union signed a non-aggression pact with Nazi Germany. The countries weren't officially allies, but they agreed not to fight each other. They also agreed to invade

---

1   Betts.

Poland together and split it up. The Nazis invaded Poland from the west on September 1, 1939, marking the beginning of the Second World War. The Soviet Union invaded from the east a few weeks later.

As it turned out, Hitler had little intention of honoring his non-aggression pact with the Soviet Union. In 1941, he broke the pact and invaded Russia. Within a month, Nazi troops advanced 500 miles.

Fast Fact: In the first four months of fighting with Nazi Germany, the Soviet army lost three million soldiers.[2]

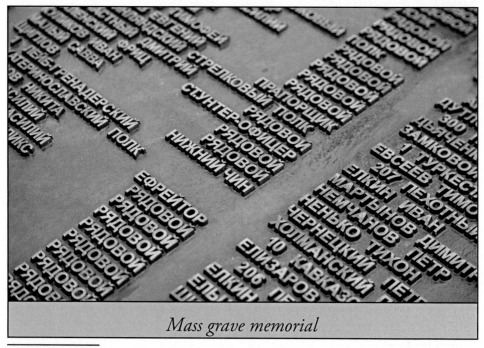

Mass grave memorial

2   Ascher, 173.

Allies, not friends

British Prime Minister Winston Churchill and American President Franklin Delano Roosevelt didn't like the Soviet Union, and Stalin didn't like them. But all three countries had the common enemy of Nazi Germany, so they agreed to work together.

In 1943, the tide of the war began to turn when Soviet troops beat the Germans at the battle of Stalingrad. A few months later, the Soviets won another key victory near Kursk, in southwestern Russia. Weapons and equipment that the Soviet Union had received from the United States and Great Britain greatly aided the Soviets in these battles.[3]

After the war

Germany finally surrendered to the allies in May 1945. The war was incredibly costly for the Soviet Union. Eight million Soviet soldiers died in battle, and another 12 million Soviet citizens died as a result of war and famine during the same time period.[4]

Despite these enormous human losses, the Soviet Union gained a lot as a result of the war. Thanks to offensives during the last few years of the war, the Soviet Union occupied six Eastern European countries as well as East Germany. Stalin hoped to install communist governments in these countries and turn them into satellite states — technically, they were independent, but the Soviet Union would strongly influence them.

3   Ascher, 174.
4   Ascher, 175.

The Cold War

The period between the end of the Second World War and the collapse of the Soviet Union would become known as the Cold War. The Cold War was a fierce rivalry between the Soviet Union and Western countries led by the United States. Despite these tensions, the two countries never fought directly.

Although the United States and the Soviet Union never fought, communist and anti-communist forces did come into conflict during the 20th century. The Russian Revolution had been the world's first attempt at communism — and it would not be the last.

The curtain and beyond

Many historians mark the official beginning of the Cold War to a speech given by former British Prime Minister Winston Churchill in 1946. Speaking in Fulton, Missouri, Churchill warned that "an iron curtain has descended" across Europe, with the Soviet Union and its satellite states on one side, and the Western capitalist countries on the other.

Churchill worried that the Soviet Union would try to expand, and he believed that Western countries had a duty to prevent the spread of communism. For the next five decades, many Western leaders would take Churchill's message to heart.

Communism in Asia

The first communist uprisings after the war took place in Asia. In China, the communist army under the leadership of Mao Zedong took down the American-backed government in 1949, following several years of fighting.

A few years later, China became involved in another conflict about communism, this time in the neighboring country of Korea. At the end of the Second World War, Korea had been divided into two parts, with the Soviet Union occupying the northern half and the United States occupying the southern half. In 1950, North Korea had invaded the South. China and the Soviet Union supported North Korea while the United States supported South Korea. The war ended in a stalemate.

The Korean War was the first of several proxy wars that would play out during the Cold War — wars where the United States and the Soviet Union fought each other through other actors. In the second half of the 20th century, both countries provided weapons, military advice, and sometimes even their own troops to opposing sides in conflicts in places as diverse as Nicaragua, Vietnam, and Afghanistan.

Fast Fact: The United States worried about a possible alliance between the Soviet Union and China, both powerful communist nations. However, Chinese premier Mao Zedong and Nikita Khrushchev — the Soviet leader who came after Stalin — did not get along well, and such a Soviet-Chinese alliance never really happened.

The nuclear question

The United States was the first country to develop nuclear weapons, using two atomic bombs in Japan to end the Second World War. As the only country with nuclear capabilities, the United States seemed to have a substantial military advantage over the rest of the world. However, the Soviet Union became a nuclear power in 1949, leveling the scales.

After 1949, the United States and the Soviet Union became engaged in an arms race, with each country trying to develop more powerful, advanced weapons. A nuclear war seemed like a real possibility.

In October 1962, the Soviet Union decided to place nuclear missiles in Cuba — a communist country located ninety miles from the United States. When American planes spotted the nuclear facilities, they raised the alarm, leading to a series of tense negotiations between Soviet and American leaders. In the end, the Soviet Union abandoned the plan to place nuclear weapons in Cuba. In exchange, the United States quietly removed its own missiles from Turkey and promised not to attack Cuba.

After Stalin

The crisis in Cuba — like the rest of the problems that the Soviet Union would face in the second half of the 20th century — was something that the country had to confront without the leadership of Josef Stalin. Stalin died in March 1953, and he did not indicate who he wanted to take his place.

At the time of Stalin's death, few people thought Nikita Khrushchev would be the many to replace him. Khrushchev had spent much of his political career working for the Communist Party in Ukraine; he was not close with Stalin. Nonetheless, he rose to become secretary of the party's Central Committee in September 1953. Later that year, Khrushchev and some of his political allies orchestrated the arrest of Lavrentiy Beria, who had named First Deputy Premier of the Soviet Union after Stalin's death. Georgi Malenkov, who had been widely seen as Stalin's heir, was forced to resign in February 1955 for his connections to Beria. While other politicians had fallen, Khrushchev managed to stay free of scandals. By the end 1955, he was the acting leader of the Soviet Union.[5]

After assuming power, Khrushchev slowly began dismantling many of Stalin's policies. While he was a committed communist, Khrushchev did not rule with an iron fist as Stalin had. Communist Party officials, who disagreed with some of his policies, removed Khrushchev from power in 1964. Perhaps as a sign of changing times, they did not kill him but allowed him to live out his days as a normal citizen.[6]

Soviet struggles

Even as the Soviet Union seemed like a global power, the country was struggling. The standard of living in the Soviet Union was much lower than in Western capitalist countries. While medical

---

5   Medlin, 143.
6   Tompson, 1101.

technology was improving across the world, the average lifespan of Soviet citizens actually declined between 1959 and 1979.[7]

It was also clear than the equality that the communists had promised did not actually exist in the Soviet Union. Some workers lived vastly better than others, and communist party officials often had luxurious homes while many families lived on incomes equivalent to less than 20 dollars per person each month.[8]

Something needed to change in the Soviet Union. Mikhail Gorbachev turned out to be the man for the job.

The End of Communism

Mikhail Gorbachev became the leader of the Soviet Union in 1985. He was 54 years old and had held important positions in the Communist Party for the previous 15 years. Gorbachev took over a country in crisis. The Soviet Union was broke — an expensive space program and a bottomless war in Afghanistan had drained the country's resources. Prices of essential goods like milk were rising rapidly, and shortages became commonplace.

Many outside economists recommended that the Soviet Union abandon government control and return to a capitalist economic system, but Gorbachev, a committed Marxist, wasn't ready for such dramatic change.

7   Ascher, 178.
8   Ascher, 178

Mikhail Gorbachev presenting his book "Alone With Myself" in Moscow House of Books on November 13, 2012.[9]

9   Photo Credit: Evgeny Eremeev / Shutterstock.com

Glasnost and Perestroika

In 1986, Gorbachev adopted a policy known as glasnost, which translates roughly to "openness." Initially, the Soviet leader seemed to mean only that the government would be more open with the public. Two years later, glasnost expanded to mean an elimination of much of the censorship that had been normal in the Soviet Union since Lenin's rule.

For the first time, Russians and other Soviet citizens were allowed to talk about Stalin's reign of terror and other forbidden subjects. They were allowed to read books that did not adhere to the Communist Party's thinking.

Gorbachev also introduced a concept called perestroika, which meant reconstruction. Perestroika encompassed several economic reforms, which allowed for some private enterprise and made trade with foreign countries easier.

These reforms were small. Gorbachev was hoping to change the Soviet Union just enough that he could save it. But his plans didn't turn out as he had anticipated.

Out-of-control freedom

Gorbachev's reforms set off a chain reaction. Citizens throughout the Soviet Union had a taste of political and economic freedom. Now, they wanted more. Rebellion broke out, beginning in the Eastern European countries that had been under Soviet rule. In 1989, the Berlin wall — the physical manifestation of Churchill's iron curtain — fell in the face of angry protestors.

The Soviet Union officially dissolved in 1991, breaking into 15 separate countries. Russia, the largest of the former Soviet member states, set on an unsteady path toward democracy and capitalism.

The Bolshevik dream of 1917 was formally over.

The Soviet Union (1922-1991) flag waving in the wind.

Conclusion

In 1917, Russia was a backwards country. For centuries, a tsar had been the only one to make decisions — the only source of political and military power. Expecting a smooth transfer from this autocratic hereditary monarchy to an equal, democratic society was probably unreasonable. Russia had no tradition of electing leaders. Peasants knew nothing of having legal rights.

Given where the country started, it's not so surprising that Russian dreams of democracy failed after the Bolsheviks took power and that the attempts for socialism likewise failed a few years later. For most of the 20th century, Russia was once again governed by an autocrat. Although the Soviet Union — with its status as a world power — looked different from the Russia of the past, the leadership of the Communist Party wasn't unlike the absolute power of the tsar.

Just as the tsar fell from power in 1917, the Soviet Union experienced its own collapse in 1991. Understanding the failure of the Russian Revolution in 1917 also provides a window into understanding Russia today. Although the collapse of the Soviet

Union gave Russia the opportunity to start on a path toward a democratic society, that path hasn't been so smooth.

Russia in 1991 had no more history of democracy than it had in 1917. Boris Yeltsin, the first president of the new Russian Federation, and his successor Vladimir Putin were both elected leaders, but some of their methods have resembled those of a traditional Russian strongman. Russian citizens do not enjoy the same rights to free speech or press that many Western citizens do. Corruption remains a serious problem.

In early 1917, protestors took to the streets because they were hungry. The chaos that followed was full of hopes and dreams, broken promises and power grabs. 100 years later, the country has undoubtedly changed. But the equal, just society that some revolutionaries dreamed of has yet to come.

Author's Note

I don't think it's a stretch to say that the Russian Revolution was one of the most pivotal events in the 20th century. Its effects were unintended and far-reaching. As it turned out, the end of a monarchy didn't create a more fair and democratic Russia, but instead threw the country into chaos. Communism, and the fear of it, shaped conflicts across the world for the next 70 years. Although the Soviet Union collapsed in 1991, the legacy of the Russian Revolution can arguably still be felt in European politics today — 100 years later — through Russia's continued struggle for democracy and conflicts over sovereignty in Eastern Europe.

The wide-ranging impacts of the Russian Revolution drew me to the topic, but history isn't just about heavy consequences. In my research for this book, I stumbled across many amusing and wild stories. Some of the events of the Russian Revolution are truly absurd, and I often found myself thinking *someone with the greatest imagination in the world couldn't make this up.*

It's tempting to laugh at Nicholas's apparent affinity for chestnuts (Chapter 1), the ridiculous nature of European alliances (Chapter 2), or incompetent Bolshevik officials who tried to use fake weapons (Chapter 6). But history isn't made up. Although the events this book described are stories to us today, they were reality for millions of Russians during the 1917 revolution and its aftermath.

History is full of unexpected lessons. Writing this book taught me about the events of the Russian Revolution. It forced me to understand Marxism better. More importantly, it made me realize that the process of writing history — like history itself — is shaped by our own biases and predispositions. Our job, as writers and readers, is to try to understand perspectives different from our own. I think if we can learn about others' motivations and goal and dreams while trying to withhold judgment, we'll understand history much better. And maybe we'll understand other things, too.

1894:

November 1: Tsar Nicholas II ascends to the Russian throne.

1903:

August: Russian socialists hold a conference in London.

1904:

February 8: Japan launches a surprise attack on the Russian naval base of Port Arthur, marking the beginning of the Russo-Japanese War.

1905:

January 9: Soldiers fire on protestors in front of the imperial palace St. Petersburg, killing many. The day would become known as "Bloody Sunday."

September 5: Russian and Japanese delegates sign the Treaty of Portsmouth, officially ending the Russo-Japanese War.

October 17: In response to the 1905 revolution, Tsar Nicholas II releases the October Manifesto, granting fundamental civil freedoms and establishing the Duma.

1914:

June 28: The heir to the Austrian throne, Archduke Franz Ferdinand, and his wife, Sophie, are assassinated in Sarajevo.

July 28: Austria-Hungary officially declares war on Serbia.

August 1: Germany declares war on Russia.

1916:

December 30: Rasputin is murdered at a dinner party hosted by Prince Felix Yusupov.

1917:

February 23: Female factory workers walk out to protest food shortages.

February 25: All major factories in Petrograd are stopped due to strikes.

February 26: Some Russian soldiers, who were called on to put down the protests, instead started a mutiny against their own commanders.

February 27: Tsar Nicholas II sets out to return to Petrograd.

February 27: The Petrograd Soviet officially forms.

March 1: The Petrograd Soviet releases Order No. 1, declaring that the military is loyal to the Soviet.

March 2: The tsar agrees to abdicate.

March 3: The Provisional Government officially forms, largely made up of former Duma members.

April 3: Vladimir Lenin arrives in Petrograd.

April 4: Lenin announces his April Theses.

June: The Russian army launches an offensive against Germany, but is quickly beaten back.

July: A series of protests known as the July Days leads to many arrests.

July 6: Alexander Kerensky is appointed the prime minister of Russia.

August: The Kornilov affair — a miscommunication or a possible coup attempt — occurs, leading Kerensky to arrest General Kornilov.

August 31: The Bolsheviks win a majority of the seats in the Petrograd Soviet.

October 9: A group called the Military Revolutionary Committee forms, with Leon Trotsky as its leader.

October 25: The Bolsheviks stage an attack on the Winter Palace, overthrowing the Provisional Government and arresting the remainder of its leaders.

October 25: The Congress of Soviets opens in Petrograd.

November: Elections for the Constituent Assembly take place, with the Bolsheviks winning only a quarter of the votes.

November 20: Germany and Russia agree to a temporary ceasefire.

December 20: The Bolsheviks establish the Cheka, a secret police.

December 27: Leon Trotsky leads a Bolshevik delegation to peace negotiations with Germany.

1918:

January: The Constituent Assembly briefly meets, but is soon dissolved by the Bolsheviks.

February: After peace negotiations don't work out, Germany launches another offensive into Russia.

March 3: German and Russian leaders sign the Treaty of Brest-Litovsk, allowing Russia to pull out of the First World War.

May: Clashes break out in the Ural Mountains between Russian soldiers and Czech soldiers traveling through Russia.

June: Lenin introduces War Communism.

July 17: The former tsar Nicholas, his family, and several of their servants are murdered.

August 30: A member of the Socialist-Revolutionary Party attempts to assassinate Lenin.

September: The Red Terror, a campaign of mass killings, begins against anyone suspected of being a Bolshevik opponent.

1919:

July: The White Army makes some impressive victories, and seems to be threatening Moscow.

October: The White Army suffers a series of defeats in southern Russia, turning the tide in favor of the Reds.

1920:

January 4: Admiral Kolchak resigns from the White Army.

April: General Denikin resigns from the White Army.

November: The White Army under Pyotr Wrangel evacuates from Crimea.

1921:

March: The Kronstadt Rebellion breaks out in response to shortages in Petrograd.

March: In response to the Kronstadt Rebellion, Lenin announces the New Economic Policy.

1922:

May: Lenin suffers his first stroke.

December 30: The Union of Soviet Socialist Republics officially forms.

1924:

January 21: Lenin dies.

1927:

November 12: Trotsky is formally expelled from the Communist Party, leaving Stalin as the undisputed leader of the Soviet Union.

1939:

September 1: Germany invades Poland, marking the beginning of the Second World War.

1940:

August 21: Trotsky is assassinated in Mexico.

1941:

June 22: Germany invades the Soviet Union, breaking the non-aggression pact.

1945:

May 7: Germany surrenders, ending the European front of the Second World War.

August 6: The United States drops an atomic bomb on the Japanese city of Hiroshima, marking the first military use of nuclear weapons.

1946:

March 5: Winston Churchill delivers his "iron curtain" speech.

1949:

August 29: The Soviet Union tests its first atomic bomb.

1953:

March 5: Josef Stalin dies.

1985:

March 11: Mikhail Gorbachev becomes the leader of the Soviet Union.

1991:

December 26: The Soviet Union officially dissolves.

2014:

March 18: Russia annexes the Crimea region, which had belonged to Ukraine since the collapse of the Soviet Union.

Bibliography

Ascher, Abraham. *The Russian Revolution*. London: One World Publications, 2014. Print.

Arno, W. F. Kolz. "British Economic Interests in Siberia during the Russian Civil War, 1918-1920." *The Journal of Modern History* 48.3 (1976): 483-491. Web.

Betts, Raymond F. "An Era of Despair." In *Europe in Retrospect*. Britannia. Web. **www.britannia.com/history/euro/3/2_2.html**.

Caillaud, Francis. "The Life and Times of Josef Stalin." Films Media Group, 1990. Web. **http://fod.infobase.com/portalplaylists.aspx?wid=104528&xtid=2563**.

Carley, Michael Jabara. "The Origins of the French Intervention in the Russian Civil War, January-May 1918: A Reappraisal." *The Journal of Modern History* 48.3 (1976): 413-439. Web.

Daly, Jonathan, and Leonid Trofimov, eds. *Russia in War and Revolution, 1914-1922: A Documentary History.* Indianapolis: Hackett Publishing Company, 2009. Print.

Dedijer, Vladimir. "Sarajevo Fifty Years After." *Foreign Affairs* 42.4 (1964): 569-584. Web.

Esthus, Raymond A. "Nicholas II and the Russo-Japanese War." *The Russian Review* 40.4 (1981): 396-411. Web.

Figes, Orlando. *A People's Tragedy: The Russian Revolution, 1891-1924.* New York: Penguin Books, 1996. Print.

Fitzpatrick, Sheila. *The Russian Revolution.* 2nd edition. New York: Oxford University Press, 1994. Print.

Hsu, Jeremy. "Lenin's Body Improves with Age." *Scientific American.* 22 Apr 2015. Web. Accessed 16 Aug 2016. **www.scientificamerican.com/article/lenin-s-body-improves-with-age1**.

"Interactive WWI Timeline." *The National WWI Museum and Memorial.* Web. Accessed 28 May 2016. **www.theworldwar.org/explore/interactive-wwi-timeline**.

Lilley, Ian, and Peter Guinness. *Russian Revolution in Color.* Films Media Group, 2005. Web. **http://fod.infobase.com/PortalPlaylists.aspx?wID=104528&xtid=42297**.

Medlin, William K. "Khrushchev: A Political Profile. III." *The Russian Review* 18.2 (1959): 131-144. Web.

Montefiore, Simon. *Young Stalin*. New York: Vintage Books, 2008. Ebook.

Pipes, Richard. "Did the Russian Revolution Have to Happen?" *The American Scholar* 63.2 (1994): 215-238. Web.

"Recognition of the Soviet Union, 1933." *U.S. State Department Office of the Historian*. Web. Accessed 13 Aug 2016. **https:// history.state.gov/milestones/1921-1936/ussr**.

Rieber, Alfred J. "Stalin, Man of the Borderlands." *The American Historical Review* 106.5 (2001): 1651-1691. Web.

Steinberg, Mark D. *Voices of Revolution, 1917*. New Haven, Yale UP, 2001. Print.

Steinberg, Mark D., and Vladimir M. Khrustalëv, *The Fall of the Romanovs: Political Dreams and Personal Struggles in a Time of Revolution*. New Haven, Yale UP, 1995. Print.

Swoboda, Victor. "Was the Soviet Union Really Necessary?" *Soviet Studies* 44.5 (1992): 761-784. Web.

Taubenberger, Jeffrey K., and David M. Morens. "1918 Influenza: the Mother of All Pandemics." *Emerging Infectious Diseases* 12.1 (January 2006): 15-22. Web. **https://wwwnc. cdc.gov/eid/article/12/1/pdfs/05-0979.pdf**.

Tompson, William J. "The Fall of Nikita Khrushchev." *Soviet Studies* 43.6 (1991): 1101-1121. Web.

Wood, Alan. *The Origins of the Russian Revolution: 1861-1917.* 2nd edition. New York: Lancaster Pamphlets, 1993. Ebook.

Wittfogel, Karl A. "The Marxist View of Russian Society and Revolution." *World Politics* 12.4 (1960): 487-508. Web.

Glossary

Abdicate: when a supreme leader steps down from his or her throne.

Anarchist: a person who opposes all forms of government.

Annexation: when one country takes land from another.

April Theses: arguments made by Lenin in a speech in April of 1917 that were later published in a newspaper. Lenin challenged the legitimacy of the Provisional Government and called for Soviet power instead.

Asiatic: relating to Asia. During the nineteenth and twentieth centuries, Europeans would use this term pejoratively to describe a society as backwards.

Atheist: a person who does not believe in any god.

Autocrat: a ruler with absolute power.

Barracks: military housing, which typically kept soldiers in tight quarters.

Bloody Sunday: the name given to the massacre of Russian protestors by the tsar's soldiers on January 9, 1905.

Bolsheviks: a name crafted by Vladimir Lenin based on the Russian word for majority, the Bolsheviks followed Lenin's brand of Marxism.

Bolshevik Central Committee: a group of top Bolshevik officials who began making most of Russia's important decisions after the October Revolution.

Bourgeoisie: in Marxist theory, the upper class that controls the means of production in an economy.

Boycott: to refuse to take part in an event or purchase a product as a form of protest.

Capitalism: an economic system based on the idea of free markets, meaning that decisions about what is produced are made by supply and demand for different goods and services, rather than a government or central organization.

Ceasefire: an agreement between militaries to temporarily or permanently stop fighting each other.

Censorship: the suppression of speech or writing that is considered objectionable.

Centrist party: a political party whose views lie in the middle of a country's political spectrum.

Civil servants: government workers or employees.

Civil war: a war between different groups within a single country.

Cheka: the secret policy in early Communist Russia.

Class consciousness: beliefs and understanding that a person holds about their social class or economic status. According to Marxist theory, the proletariat had to develop a class consciousness before a Marxist revolution could occur.

Coalition government: a government in which no single political party has the majority, so different parties have to form alliances and work together.

Cold War: the period between the end of the Second World War and the collapse of the Soviet Union, characterized by tense relations between capitalist countries (led by the United States) and communist countries (led by the Soviet Union).

Collectivization: a Soviet agricultural policy which created group farms for peasants instead of individual ones.

Commissariat of War: the head of the military, in early Bolshevik Russia, this was Trotsky's position.

Commodification: valuing some things only for economic purposes.

Communism: an economic system where the means of production are owned communally and decisions about what to produce are made by a central governing power.

Comrade: to eliminate a hierarchy of power, Marxists always referred to each other as comrades.

Congress: a political meeting.

Constitutional Democrats: a centrist party in Russia prior to the 1917 revolution; its members were called Kadets.

Cossacks: units of Russian soldiers who were known to be tough, skilled fighters.

Currency: physical objects (for example, coins or bills) that are used as a medium of exchange for goods and services.

Defect: to leave one army and join another.

Desert: to leave the military without permission.

Draft: government selection of individuals for mandatory military service.

Duma: the Russian word for council. Between 1905 and 1917, the Russian national Duma served as a legislative body, although it lacked significant power. Local towns also had their own dumas.

Emancipation of the Russian Serfs: an order by Russia's Tsar Alexander II in 1861that ended Russia's official system that bound workers to their landlords.

Fascism: a political ideology focused around nationalism and loyalty to the state.

Glasnost: a policy of openness implemented under Mikhail Gorbachev, which eventually led to relaxing much of the Soviet Union's censorship.

Green armies: peasant armies during the Russian Civil War, who aligned with neither the Reds nor the Whites.

Gregorian Calendar: the modern-day calendar, which Russia adopted in 1918.

Guerilla warfare: the use of surprise raids and secret, small attacks in order to achieve military goals.

Hemophilia: a genetic disorder that prevents blood clotting.

Hemophilic: describing someone with hemophilia.

Hereditary monarchy: a system of government in which power is passed down from one relative to the next.

House of Romanov: the line of Russian hereditary rulers who governed the country from 1613 until 1917.

House of Special Designation: the name the Bolsheviks used for the building in the Ural Mountains where Tsar Nicholas II and his family were executed.

Imperial rule: government led by a hereditary monarch.

Indemnity: payment that a country that loses a war must pay to a country that wins a war.

Inflation: an increase in the price level for goods and services in an economy.

Industrial Proletariat: the working class.

July Days: a series of uprisings against the Provisional Government in July 1917.

July Ultimatum: a series of demands issued by the Austro-Hungary empire to the government of Serbia in retaliation for the assassination of Archduke Franz Ferdinand.

Julian Calendar: an old-style calendar that Russia used until 1918.

Kadet: a member of the Constitutional Democrats.

Kronstadt Rebellion: an uprising against the communist government by soldiers at the Kronstadt military base in March 1921.

Kulak: a term describing well-to-do Russian peasants.

Labor Group: a left-wing party that won a number of seats in Russia's first Duma, but was considered too radical by Tsar Nicholas II.

Law of Succession: a Russian rule that dictated how power passed from one monarch to the next.

Malnutrition: a health problem resulting from a lack of food.

Manifesto on the Improvement of the State Order: the October Manifesto issued by Tsar Nicholas II in response to the 1905 revolution.

Means of production: in Marxist theory, the materials in an economy that are used to produce other goods.

Mensheviks: Lenin gave his Marxist opponents this name based on the Russian word for minority. Mensheviks opposed some of Lenin's ideas about party structure.

Military Revolutionary Committee: a group led by Trotsky that had the official goal of protecting Russia from a German invasion, but actually planned and carried out the October Revolution.

Mir: a village council in rural Russia prior to the Revolution.

Nationalization: the act of bringing an industry or a particular part of a country's economy under the control of the government.

New Economic Policy: a plan introduced by Vladimir Lenin in 1921 that allowed for some private enterprise in Russia, with a goal of stimulating economic growth.

October Manifesto: also known as the Manifesto on the Improvement of the State Order. Tsar Nicholas II issued the manifesto in response to the 1905 revolution. It granted many civil freedoms and called for the establishment of the Duma.

Octobrist: a member of the Union of 17 October Party, a centrist party in Russia prior to 1917.

Okhrana: the imperial tsar's secret police.

Pavlovsky Regiment: one of the first army groups to fight back against its commanders during the February Revolution.

Peasant: a person in Russia who worked in agriculture and was of a poor economic background.

Perestroika: policy of restructuring implemented under Mikhail Gorbachev, which eventually led to the allowance of some private enterprise.

Petrograd Soviet of Workers' and Soldiers' Deputies: a group of 5,000 elected workers and soldiers who convened in the midst of the February Revolution with the hope of governing a new Russia. Its name would later be shortened to Petrograd Soviet.

Platform: a political party's official list of goals and ideas.

Politburo: a high-ranking group of communist officials who were responsible for most of the Soviet Union's decision making.

Political consciousness: beliefs and understanding that a person holds about their role in the world. According to Karl Marx, consciousness — people's awareness of themselves — was always political, because political situations shaped how people viewed themselves.

Private enterprise: people producing, buying, and selling goods from one another under a capitalist economic system.

Prodrazvyorstka: a component of Lenin's War Communism that required peasants to give certain amount of grain and agricultural produce to the government.

Provisional Executive Committee of the Soviet of Workers' Deputies: the initial name for a group of workers, soldiers, and politicians who organized during the February Revolution. The group called for elections or workers and soldiers that eventually created the Petrograd Soviet.

Proxy war: a conflict between two countries where neither directly fights the other one.

Purge: a mass, violent removal of people, usually for political reasons.

Rabochii Put: a Bolshevik newspaper that was shut down by the Provisional Government on October 24, 1917.

Rationing: restrictions on the quantity of essential goods (like food) that people can buy, usually due to crises like war or shortages.

Red Army: the communist government's army during the Russian Civil War.

Red Guards: armed groups of workers and soldiers that helped the Bolsheviks achieve their military goals during the October Revolution.

Red Terror: a campaign of mass killing and torture by the communist government with a goal of rooting out opposition.

Reds: pro-government forces during the Russian Civil War.

Referendum: a yes/no vote.

Russian Social Democratic Labor Party (RSDRP): an early Russian socialist political party, founded in 1898.

Satellite states: countries that are formally independent but are strongly influenced by another country.

Secede: to withdraw from a political body.

Seminary: a school for the study of religion.

Serfs: workers bound to work exclusively for their landlord.

Single-party state: a country where all political positions are held by members of a certain political party.

State terror: government-approved violence used to advance some political purpose.

Social-Revolutionaries (SR) Party: a Russian political party founded in 1900 that advocated land redistribution.

Socialism: an economic system where the goods and services produced are shared equally by everyone in the economy.

Temporary Committee of Duma Members for the Restoration of Order in the Capital and the Establishment of Relations with Individuals and Institutions: the initial group of Duma members that formed after the tsar's abdication and later evolved into the Provisional Government.

Treason: a violation of allegiance to one's country.

Treaty of Brest-Litovsk: signed on March 3, 1918, the treaty between Germany and Russia that ended Russia's involvement in the First World War.

Treaty of Portsmouth: signed on September 5, 1905, the treaty formally ended the Russo-Japanese war.

Treaty of Versailles: signed on June 28, 1919, the treaty formally ended the First World War.

Union of 17 October Party: a centrist party in Russia prior to 1917.

War Communism: a policy enacted by Vladimir Lenin in June of 1918 that attempted to increase Russia's economic production by bringing many industries under government control. War Communism failed to achieve its goal of increased output.

White Army: the military groups fighting against the communist government during the Russian Civil War.

Whites: during the Russian Civil War, the coalition of groups opposing the communist government.

Index

About the Author

Jessica E. Piper is an American writer and researcher. In 2013, she was recognized as a National Endowment for the Humanities Scholar for her research on changing American labor relations in the late 1800s. She has also researched diaspora settlement history at the Jewish Museum of Hohenems in Hohenems, Austria, and has written about contemporary immigration issues for several magazines. She is currently studying economics and works as a news editor for a weekly college newspaper.